50 Fusion Street Food Recipes for Home

By: Kelly Johnson

Table of Contents

- Sushi Burrito
- Korean BBQ Tacos
- Ramen Burger
- Indian Butter Chicken Pizza
- Thai Green Curry Tacos
- Falafel Waffle
- Pad Thai Nachos
- Jerk Chicken Quesadilla
- Kimchi Quesadilla
- Teriyaki Chicken Sliders
- Banh Mi Hot Dog
- BBQ Pulled Pork Tacos
- Naan Pizza
- Tempura Fish Tacos
- Peruvian Lomo Saltado Fries
- Bulgogi Beef Tacos
- Shawarma Pizza
- Vietnamese Banh Xeo Tacos
- General Tso's Chicken Burrito
- Tandoori Chicken Tacos
- Korean Fried Chicken Waffle
- Thai Peanut Noodles Burrito
- Gyro Fries
- Tikka Masala Burrito
- Ramen Tacos
- Kimchi Fried Rice Burrito
- Pad Thai Pizza
- Falafel Tacos
- Bulgogi Burger
- Chicken Tikka Masala Pizza
- Tempura Shrimp Po' Boy
- Sushi Pizza
- BBQ Pork Belly Tacos
- Peruvian Chicken Empanadas
- Shawarma Burrito

- Thai Basil Chicken Waffle
- Korean BBQ Pizza
- Banh Mi Burger
- General Tso's Chicken Tacos
- Teriyaki Salmon Poke Bowl
- Naan Tacos
- Jerk Chicken Sliders
- Tempura Chicken Waffle
- Kimchi Fries
- Indian Samosa Tacos
- Bulgogi Beef Sliders
- Sushi Nachos
- Pad Thai Burrito
- Banh Mi Tacos
- BBQ Pulled Jackfruit Sandwich

Sushi Burrito

Ingredients:

- 2 sheets of nori (seaweed)
- 2 cups cooked sushi rice
- 1/2 lb (225g) sushi-grade raw fish (such as tuna or salmon), thinly sliced
- 1/2 cucumber, julienned
- 1/2 avocado, sliced
- 1/4 cup shredded carrots
- 1/4 cup shredded red cabbage
- 1/4 cup sliced radishes
- 2 tablespoons pickled ginger
- 2 tablespoons soy sauce
- 2 tablespoons sesame seeds
- Wasabi and/or sriracha mayo (optional, for extra flavor)

Instructions:

1. Prepare Ingredients:
    - Cook sushi rice according to package instructions and let it cool to room temperature.
    - Slice the raw fish into thin strips.
    - Julienne the cucumber and slice the avocado.
    - Shred the carrots and red cabbage.
    - Slice the radishes thinly.
2. Assemble the Sushi Burrito:
    - Place a sheet of nori on a clean surface, with the shiny side facing down.
    - Spread half of the cooked sushi rice evenly over the nori, leaving about an inch of space at the top edge.
    - Arrange the sliced raw fish, cucumber, avocado, shredded carrots, shredded red cabbage, sliced radishes, and pickled ginger in the center of the rice.
3. Roll the Burrito:
    - Start rolling the nori and rice over the filling, using a sushi mat or your hands to tightly roll it into a burrito shape.
    - Wet the top inch of the nori with water to seal the edge.

- Repeat the process with the second sheet of nori and remaining ingredients.
4. Slice and Serve:
    - Use a sharp knife to slice each sushi burrito in half or into smaller pieces.
    - Serve with soy sauce for dipping, and sprinkle sesame seeds over the top for extra flavor.
    - Optional: Serve with wasabi and/or sriracha mayo on the side for dipping or drizzling over the sushi burrito.
5. Enjoy:
    - Enjoy your homemade Sushi Burrito immediately, or wrap it tightly in plastic wrap and refrigerate until ready to eat.

This Sushi Burrito is a fun and portable way to enjoy your favorite sushi flavors on the go! Feel free to customize the fillings according to your taste preferences.

Korean BBQ Tacos

Ingredients:

For the Korean BBQ Beef:

- 1 lb (450g) beef sirloin or flank steak, thinly sliced
- 1/4 cup soy sauce
- 2 tablespoons brown sugar
- 2 tablespoons rice vinegar
- 2 tablespoons sesame oil
- 2 cloves garlic, minced
- 1 teaspoon grated ginger
- 1 tablespoon sesame seeds
- 2 green onions, thinly sliced
- 1 tablespoon vegetable oil, for cooking

For the Tacos:

- 8 small flour or corn tortillas
- Kimchi, for topping
- 1 cup shredded lettuce or cabbage
- 1/2 cup matchstick carrots
- 1/4 cup chopped fresh cilantro
- Sriracha mayo or gochujang sauce, for drizzling (optional)

Instructions:

1. Marinate the Beef:
    - In a bowl, whisk together the soy sauce, brown sugar, rice vinegar, sesame oil, minced garlic, grated ginger, sesame seeds, and sliced green onions.
    - Add the thinly sliced beef to the marinade, making sure it's well coated. Cover and refrigerate for at least 30 minutes, or up to 4 hours.
2. Cook the Beef:
    - Heat vegetable oil in a large skillet or grill pan over medium-high heat.
    - Remove the beef from the marinade, allowing excess marinade to drip off. Discard the marinade.

- Cook the beef slices in the skillet for 2-3 minutes per side, or until browned and cooked to your desired level of doneness.
3. Prepare the Toppings:
    - Warm the tortillas in a dry skillet or microwave.
    - Prepare the toppings: shred lettuce or cabbage, chop cilantro, and gather kimchi and matchstick carrots.
4. Assemble the Tacos:
    - Place a few slices of cooked Korean BBQ beef on each tortilla.
    - Top with shredded lettuce or cabbage, matchstick carrots, kimchi, and chopped cilantro.
    - Drizzle with sriracha mayo or gochujang sauce, if desired.
5. Serve:
    - Serve the Korean BBQ Tacos immediately, with lime wedges on the side for squeezing.
    - Enjoy these flavorful tacos as a delicious and unique meal!

Feel free to customize the toppings and adjust the spiciness level according to your taste preferences. These Korean BBQ Tacos are sure to be a hit at your next taco night!

Ramen Burger

Ingredients:

For the Ramen Buns:

- 2 packages of instant ramen noodles (any flavor)
- 2 large eggs
- Cooking spray or vegetable oil

For the Burger Patties:

- 1 lb (450g) ground beef
- 2 tablespoons soy sauce
- 2 cloves garlic, minced
- 1 teaspoon grated ginger
- Salt and pepper to taste

For the Burger Toppings:

- Sliced cheese (cheddar, American, or your choice)
- Lettuce leaves
- Sliced tomatoes
- Sliced onions
- Mayonnaise, ketchup, mustard, or your preferred condiments

Instructions:

1. Prepare the Ramen Buns:
    - Cook the instant ramen noodles according to the package instructions, but do not add the seasoning packets. Drain the noodles and let them cool slightly.
    - In a large bowl, beat the eggs. Add the cooked ramen noodles to the beaten eggs and mix until well combined.

- Divide the ramen mixture into 4 equal portions. Shape each portion into a bun-sized patty, about 1/2 inch thick.
- Heat a skillet or griddle over medium heat and lightly grease it with cooking spray or vegetable oil. Cook the ramen buns for 3-4 minutes on each side, or until golden brown and crispy. Remove from the skillet and set aside.

2. Prepare the Burger Patties:
   - In a mixing bowl, combine the ground beef, soy sauce, minced garlic, grated ginger, salt, and pepper. Mix until well combined.
   - Divide the beef mixture into 4 equal portions. Shape each portion into a burger patty, slightly larger than the ramen buns to account for shrinkage during cooking.
   - Heat the same skillet or griddle over medium-high heat. Cook the burger patties for 3-4 minutes on each side, or until they reach your desired level of doneness. Add sliced cheese to the patties during the last minute of cooking, if desired, and let it melt.

3. Assemble the Ramen Burgers:
   - Place a cooked ramen bun on a plate. Top it with a cooked burger patty.
   - Add your desired toppings, such as lettuce, tomato slices, onion slices, and condiments.
   - Top with another ramen bun.
   - Repeat the process to assemble the remaining burgers.

4. Serve:
   - Serve the Ramen Burgers immediately, while the ramen buns are still crispy.
   - Enjoy this unique and flavorful twist on a classic burger!

Feel free to customize your Ramen Burgers with your favorite burger toppings and condiments. They're sure to be a hit at any gathering or dinner table!

Indian Butter Chicken Pizza

Ingredients:

For the Butter Chicken:

- 1 lb (450g) boneless, skinless chicken breasts, cut into bite-sized pieces
- 1/4 cup plain yogurt
- 2 tablespoons lemon juice
- 2 cloves garlic, minced
- 1 teaspoon grated ginger
- 1 teaspoon ground cumin
- 1 teaspoon ground coriander
- 1/2 teaspoon turmeric
- 1/2 teaspoon paprika
- 1/4 teaspoon cayenne pepper (adjust to taste)
- Salt to taste
- 2 tablespoons butter
- 1 small onion, finely chopped
- 1 cup tomato puree
- 1/2 cup heavy cream
- 2 tablespoons chopped fresh cilantro (coriander)

For the Pizza:

- 1 pre-made pizza dough or homemade pizza dough
- 1 cup shredded mozzarella cheese
- 1/4 cup crumbled paneer cheese (optional)
- 1/4 cup chopped fresh cilantro (coriander)
- Naan or pita bread, for serving (optional)

Instructions:

1. Marinate the Chicken:
    - In a bowl, combine the plain yogurt, lemon juice, minced garlic, grated ginger, ground cumin, ground coriander, turmeric, paprika, cayenne pepper, and salt. Mix well.

- Add the bite-sized chicken pieces to the marinade and toss to coat. Cover and refrigerate for at least 30 minutes, or up to 4 hours.

2. Cook the Butter Chicken:
    - In a large skillet or pan, melt the butter over medium heat. Add the finely chopped onion and cook until softened and translucent, about 5 minutes.
    - Add the marinated chicken pieces along with any excess marinade to the skillet. Cook until the chicken is browned and cooked through, about 8-10 minutes.
    - Stir in the tomato puree and heavy cream. Simmer the mixture for another 5-10 minutes, stirring occasionally, until the sauce has thickened.
    - Stir in the chopped fresh cilantro (coriander). Remove from heat and set aside.

3. Prepare the Pizza:
    - Preheat your oven to the temperature recommended for your pizza dough.
    - Roll out the pizza dough on a floured surface to your desired thickness. Place the rolled-out dough on a pizza pan or baking sheet lined with parchment paper.
    - Spread a layer of the prepared butter chicken over the pizza dough, leaving a small border around the edges.
    - Sprinkle shredded mozzarella cheese over the butter chicken layer. Optionally, sprinkle crumbled paneer cheese over the top.
    - Bake the pizza in the preheated oven according to the instructions for your pizza dough, until the crust is golden brown and the cheese is melted and bubbly.

4. Serve:
    - Remove the Indian Butter Chicken Pizza from the oven and sprinkle chopped fresh cilantro (coriander) over the top.
    - Slice the pizza and serve it hot. Optionally, serve with naan or pita bread on the side for dipping in the extra butter chicken sauce.

Enjoy the delicious fusion of Indian flavors and pizza with this Indian Butter Chicken Pizza! It's perfect for a unique and flavorful meal.

Thai Green Curry Tacos

Ingredients:

For the Thai Green Curry:

- 1 tablespoon vegetable oil
- 2 tablespoons Thai green curry paste
- 1 can (13.5 oz / 400ml) coconut milk
- 1 tablespoon fish sauce (or soy sauce for a vegetarian option)
- 1 tablespoon brown sugar
- 1 cup sliced vegetables (such as bell peppers, carrots, and snap peas)
- 1 cup cooked protein (such as sliced chicken, shrimp, tofu, or tempeh)
- Fresh cilantro leaves, for garnish
- Lime wedges, for serving

For the Tacos:

- 8 small flour or corn tortillas
- Sliced cucumber, for topping
- Sliced red onion, for topping
- Sliced jalapeños, for topping
- Chopped peanuts, for topping
- Sriracha or chili sauce, for drizzling (optional)

Instructions:

1. Prepare the Thai Green Curry:
    - Heat the vegetable oil in a large skillet or wok over medium heat.
    - Add the Thai green curry paste and cook for 1-2 minutes, stirring constantly, until fragrant.
    - Pour in the coconut milk and stir until the curry paste is fully incorporated.
    - Stir in the fish sauce (or soy sauce) and brown sugar.
    - Add the sliced vegetables and cooked protein to the skillet. Cook for 3-4 minutes, or until the vegetables are tender and the protein is heated through.
2. Warm the Tortillas:

- Meanwhile, warm the tortillas in a dry skillet or microwave until soft and pliable.
3. Assemble the Tacos:
    - Spoon the Thai green curry mixture onto each tortilla.
    - Top with sliced cucumber, red onion, jalapeños, chopped peanuts, and fresh cilantro leaves.
    - Drizzle with sriracha or chili sauce, if desired.
4. Serve:
    - Serve the Thai Green Curry Tacos immediately, with lime wedges on the side for squeezing.
    - Enjoy the flavorful combination of Thai green curry and tacos!

Feel free to customize the toppings and adjust the spiciness level according to your taste preferences. These Thai Green Curry Tacos are sure to be a hit at your next taco night!

Falafel Waffle

Ingredients:

- 1 cup dried chickpeas (garbanzo beans), soaked overnight
- 1/2 small onion, chopped
- 2 cloves garlic, minced
- 1/4 cup fresh parsley, chopped
- 1/4 cup fresh cilantro, chopped
- 1 teaspoon ground cumin
- 1 teaspoon ground coriander
- 1/2 teaspoon baking powder
- 1 tablespoon all-purpose flour or chickpea flour (for a gluten-free option)
- Salt and pepper to taste
- Cooking spray or olive oil, for greasing the waffle iron

For Serving:

- Pita bread or flatbread
- Hummus
- Tzatziki sauce or tahini sauce
- Chopped tomatoes
- Chopped cucumbers
- Chopped lettuce or arugula
- Sliced red onion
- Lemon wedges
- Optional: crumbled feta cheese, olives, hot sauce

Instructions:

1. Prepare the Falafel Batter:
    - Drain the soaked chickpeas and pat them dry with a clean kitchen towel.
    - In a food processor, combine the soaked chickpeas, chopped onion, minced garlic, fresh parsley, fresh cilantro, ground cumin, ground coriander, baking powder, flour, salt, and pepper. Pulse until the mixture is finely ground and holds together when pressed.

2. Cook the Falafel Waffle:
    - Preheat your waffle iron according to the manufacturer's instructions.
    - Lightly grease the waffle iron with cooking spray or brush with olive oil.
    - Spoon the falafel mixture onto the preheated waffle iron, spreading it out evenly to cover the surface. Close the lid and cook for 5-7 minutes, or until the falafel waffle is golden brown and crisp.
    - Carefully remove the falafel waffle from the waffle iron and repeat with the remaining falafel mixture.
3. Assemble the Falafel Waffle:
    - Serve the falafel waffle hot with your choice of accompaniments, such as pita bread or flatbread, hummus, tzatziki sauce or tahini sauce, chopped tomatoes, chopped cucumbers, chopped lettuce or arugula, sliced red onion, and lemon wedges.
    - Garnish with crumbled feta cheese, olives, and hot sauce if desired.
4. Enjoy:
    - Enjoy your Falafel Waffle as a delicious and unique twist on the classic falafel sandwich!

This Falafel Waffle is crispy on the outside and tender on the inside, making it a satisfying and flavorful meal. Feel free to customize the toppings and accompaniments to suit your taste preferences.

Pad Thai Nachos

Ingredients:

For the Pad Thai Sauce:

- 1/4 cup soy sauce
- 2 tablespoons tamarind paste
- 2 tablespoons brown sugar
- 2 tablespoons fish sauce (or vegetarian/vegan alternative)
- 1 tablespoon rice vinegar
- 1 teaspoon Sriracha sauce (adjust to taste)

For the Nachos:

- 1 bag (about 8 oz) tortilla chips
- 2 cups cooked chicken breast, shredded (or substitute tofu for vegetarian/vegan option)
- 1 cup bean sprouts
- 1/2 cup shredded carrots
- 1/2 cup chopped green onions
- 1/4 cup chopped peanuts
- 1/4 cup chopped fresh cilantro
- Lime wedges, for serving

Instructions:

1. Prepare the Pad Thai Sauce:
    - In a small saucepan, combine the soy sauce, tamarind paste, brown sugar, fish sauce, rice vinegar, and Sriracha sauce.
    - Heat the mixture over medium heat, stirring occasionally, until the sugar has dissolved and the sauce is well combined. Set aside.
2. Assemble the Nachos:
    - Preheat your oven to 350°F (175°C).
    - Arrange the tortilla chips in a single layer on a large baking sheet or oven-safe serving platter.

- Sprinkle the shredded chicken (or tofu) evenly over the tortilla chips.
- Drizzle the prepared Pad Thai sauce over the chicken and tortilla chips, ensuring that all the chips are coated evenly.
- Sprinkle the bean sprouts, shredded carrots, and chopped green onions over the top of the nachos.

3. Bake the Nachos:
   - Place the baking sheet or platter in the preheated oven and bake for 10-12 minutes, or until the nachos are heated through and the edges of the tortilla chips are slightly crispy.
4. Garnish and Serve:
   - Remove the nachos from the oven and sprinkle the chopped peanuts and fresh cilantro over the top.
   - Serve the Pad Thai Nachos immediately, accompanied by lime wedges for squeezing over the nachos.
   - Enjoy these flavorful and unique nachos as a delicious appetizer or main dish!

Feel free to customize the toppings according to your preferences. You can also add additional ingredients such as chopped bell peppers, sliced jalapeños, or shredded cabbage for extra flavor and texture. Enjoy your Pad Thai Nachos!

Jerk Chicken Quesadilla

Ingredients:

For the Jerk Chicken:

- 2 boneless, skinless chicken breasts
- 2 tablespoons jerk seasoning
- 2 tablespoons olive oil

For the Quesadilla:

- 4 large flour tortillas
- 2 cups shredded Monterey Jack cheese
- 1 cup diced pineapple
- 1/4 cup thinly sliced red onion
- 1/4 cup chopped fresh cilantro
- 1 lime, cut into wedges (for serving)
- Sour cream, salsa, or guacamole (for serving)

Instructions:

1. Prepare the Jerk Chicken:
    - Rub the jerk seasoning all over the chicken breasts, ensuring they are evenly coated.
    - Heat olive oil in a skillet over medium-high heat. Cook the chicken breasts for 6-7 minutes per side, or until cooked through and nicely charred. Remove from heat and let them rest for a few minutes before slicing them thinly.
2. Assemble the Quesadilla:
    - Heat a large skillet or griddle over medium heat.
    - Place one tortilla in the skillet. Sprinkle half of the shredded cheese evenly over the tortilla.
    - Arrange half of the sliced jerk chicken, diced pineapple, red onion slices, and chopped cilantro over the cheese.
    - Sprinkle the remaining cheese over the top, and cover with another tortilla.

- Cook the quesadilla for 3-4 minutes on each side, or until the tortilla is golden brown and the cheese is melted and gooey. Repeat with the remaining tortillas and filling ingredients.
3. Serve:
    - Cut the cooked quesadillas into wedges and serve hot.
    - Serve with lime wedges and your choice of sour cream, salsa, or guacamole on the side for dipping.

Enjoy the delicious fusion of Caribbean and Mexican flavors in this Jerk Chicken Quesadilla! It's perfect for a quick and tasty meal or snack.

Kimchi Quesadilla

Ingredients:

- 2 large flour tortillas
- 1 cup shredded Monterey Jack cheese
- 1 cup kimchi, drained and chopped
- 2 green onions, thinly sliced
- 1 tablespoon vegetable oil, for cooking
- Sour cream or Greek yogurt, for serving (optional)
- Sriracha or hot sauce, for serving (optional)

Instructions:

1. Prepare the Quesadilla:
    - Heat a large skillet or griddle over medium heat.
    - Place one flour tortilla in the skillet. Sprinkle half of the shredded Monterey Jack cheese evenly over the tortilla.
    - Spread the chopped kimchi over the cheese, then sprinkle the sliced green onions on top.
    - Sprinkle the remaining cheese evenly over the kimchi and green onions.
    - Place the second flour tortilla on top to cover the filling.
2. Cook the Quesadilla:
    - Drizzle a little vegetable oil into the skillet around the edges of the quesadilla.
    - Cook the quesadilla for 2-3 minutes on each side, or until the tortillas are golden brown and crispy and the cheese is melted and gooey. Press down gently with a spatula while cooking to help seal the quesadilla together.
3. Serve:
    - Once cooked, transfer the quesadilla to a cutting board and let it cool for a minute or two.
    - Cut the quesadilla into wedges using a sharp knife or pizza cutter.
    - Serve hot, with sour cream or Greek yogurt and sriracha or hot sauce on the side for dipping, if desired.

Enjoy the unique and flavorful combination of kimchi and melted cheese in this Kimchi Quesadilla! It's perfect for a quick and satisfying meal or snack.

Teriyaki Chicken Sliders

Ingredients:

For the Teriyaki Chicken:

- 1 lb (about 450g) boneless, skinless chicken thighs or breasts
- 1/2 cup teriyaki sauce (store-bought or homemade)
- 2 cloves garlic, minced
- 1 tablespoon grated ginger
- 2 tablespoons vegetable oil
- Salt and pepper, to taste

For the Sliders:

- Slider buns or dinner rolls
- Sliced pineapple rings
- Sliced red onion
- Lettuce leaves
- Mayonnaise (optional)
- Sriracha or hot sauce (optional)
- Toothpicks, for securing

Instructions:

1. Prepare the Teriyaki Chicken:
    - In a bowl, whisk together the teriyaki sauce, minced garlic, and grated ginger.
    - Cut the chicken thighs or breasts into small pieces suitable for sliders.
    - Season the chicken pieces with salt and pepper to taste.
    - Heat vegetable oil in a skillet over medium-high heat. Add the chicken pieces to the skillet and cook until browned and cooked through, about 4-5 minutes per side.
    - Pour the teriyaki sauce mixture over the cooked chicken in the skillet. Allow the sauce to simmer and thicken, coating the chicken evenly. Remove from heat.

2. Assemble the Sliders:
    - Slice the slider buns or dinner rolls in half horizontally.
    - Place a lettuce leaf on the bottom half of each bun.
    - Top with a piece of teriyaki chicken, followed by a slice of pineapple and a slice of red onion.
    - If desired, spread mayonnaise and/or drizzle sriracha or hot sauce on the top half of each bun.
    - Place the top half of the bun over the filling ingredients.
    - Secure each slider with a toothpick to hold everything together.
3. Serve:
    - Arrange the Teriyaki Chicken Sliders on a serving platter and serve immediately.
    - Enjoy these flavorful sliders as a delicious appetizer, snack, or meal!

These Teriyaki Chicken Sliders are sure to be a hit at any gathering or party. They're easy to make and packed with delicious flavors!

Banh Mi Hot Dog

Ingredients:

For the Banh Mi Hot Dogs:

- 4 hot dog buns
- 4 hot dogs
- 1 cup pickled vegetables (carrots, daikon radish, and cucumber)
- 1/4 cup fresh cilantro leaves
- 2 green onions, thinly sliced
- Sriracha mayo (mix sriracha sauce with mayonnaise to taste)
- Hoisin sauce
- Soy sauce
- Vegetable oil, for cooking

For the Pickled Vegetables:

- 1 cup julienned carrots
- 1 cup julienned daikon radish
- 1 cup thinly sliced cucumber
- 1/2 cup rice vinegar
- 1/4 cup water
- 2 tablespoons sugar
- 1 teaspoon salt

Instructions:

1. Prepare the Pickled Vegetables:
    - In a bowl, mix together the rice vinegar, water, sugar, and salt until the sugar and salt dissolve.
    - Add the julienned carrots, daikon radish, and sliced cucumber to the vinegar mixture, making sure they are submerged.
    - Cover and refrigerate for at least 1 hour, or overnight, to allow the vegetables to pickle.
2. Cook the Hot Dogs:

- Heat a grill or grill pan over medium-high heat.
- Grill the hot dogs for 5-7 minutes, turning occasionally, until they are heated through and have grill marks. Alternatively, you can boil or pan-fry the hot dogs according to your preference.

3. Assemble the Banh Mi Hot Dogs:
   - Toast the hot dog buns on the grill or in a toaster until lightly golden.
   - Place a hot dog in each toasted bun.
   - Drizzle each hot dog with hoisin sauce and soy sauce, to taste.
   - Top each hot dog with a generous amount of pickled vegetables, fresh cilantro leaves, and sliced green onions.
   - Drizzle sriracha mayo over the top of each hot dog.
4. Serve:
   - Serve the Banh Mi Hot Dogs immediately, accompanied by extra sriracha mayo, hoisin sauce, and soy sauce on the side for dipping, if desired.
   - Enjoy the fusion of flavors in these delicious Banh Mi Hot Dogs!

These Banh Mi Hot Dogs are a fun twist on the classic Vietnamese sandwich, packed with flavor and perfect for a summer cookout or casual meal.

BBQ Pulled Pork Tacos

Ingredients:

For the BBQ Pulled Pork:

- 2 lbs (about 900g) pork shoulder or pork butt
- Salt and pepper, to taste
- 1 cup barbecue sauce (store-bought or homemade)
- 1/2 cup chicken broth or water
- 2 cloves garlic, minced
- 1 onion, chopped
- 1 tablespoon vegetable oil

For the Tacos:

- 12 small corn or flour tortillas
- 1 cup shredded lettuce
- 1 cup diced tomatoes
- 1/2 cup diced red onion
- 1/2 cup chopped fresh cilantro
- Lime wedges, for serving

Instructions:

1. Prepare the BBQ Pulled Pork:
    - Season the pork shoulder or pork butt with salt and pepper on all sides.
    - Heat vegetable oil in a large skillet or Dutch oven over medium-high heat.
    - Brown the pork on all sides until golden brown, about 3-4 minutes per side.
    - Transfer the browned pork to a slow cooker.
    - In the same skillet or Dutch oven, sauté the minced garlic and chopped onion until softened and fragrant, about 2-3 minutes.
    - Add the sautéed garlic and onion to the slow cooker.
    - Pour the barbecue sauce and chicken broth (or water) over the pork in the slow cooker, making sure the pork is well coated.

- Cover and cook on low heat for 8-10 hours, or until the pork is tender and easily shreds with a fork.
2. Shred the Pork:
    - Once the pork is cooked, remove it from the slow cooker and transfer it to a cutting board.
    - Use two forks to shred the pork into bite-sized pieces.
3. Assemble the Tacos:
    - Warm the tortillas in a dry skillet or microwave until soft and pliable.
    - Fill each tortilla with a generous portion of the shredded BBQ pulled pork.
    - Top the pulled pork with shredded lettuce, diced tomatoes, diced red onion, and chopped fresh cilantro.
    - Squeeze a lime wedge over each taco for a burst of freshness.
4. Serve:
    - Serve the BBQ Pulled Pork Tacos immediately, with extra barbecue sauce and lime wedges on the side for drizzling, if desired.
    - Enjoy these flavorful and satisfying tacos for a delicious meal!

These BBQ Pulled Pork Tacos are perfect for a casual dinner or for entertaining guests.

They're easy to make and packed with delicious flavors!

Naan Pizza

Ingredients:

- 4 pieces of naan bread
- 1 cup pizza sauce
- 2 cups shredded mozzarella cheese
- Your choice of toppings (e.g., pepperoni, bell peppers, onions, mushrooms, olives, cooked chicken, cooked sausage, etc.)
- Olive oil, for brushing
- Optional: fresh basil leaves, grated Parmesan cheese, red pepper flakes

Instructions:

1. Preheat the Oven:
    - Preheat your oven to 425°F (220°C).
2. Prepare the Naan:
    - Place the naan bread on a baking sheet lined with parchment paper.
    - Lightly brush the tops of the naan bread with olive oil.
3. Assemble the Pizzas:
    - Spread a layer of pizza sauce evenly over each naan bread, leaving a small border around the edges.
    - Sprinkle shredded mozzarella cheese over the sauce.
    - Add your desired toppings evenly over the cheese.
4. Bake the Pizzas:
    - Place the baking sheet in the preheated oven.
    - Bake for 10-12 minutes, or until the cheese is melted and bubbly, and the edges of the naan are golden brown.
5. Serve:
    - Remove the naan pizzas from the oven.
    - Optional: sprinkle with fresh basil leaves, grated Parmesan cheese, or red pepper flakes for extra flavor.
    - Slice the naan pizzas into wedges or squares and serve hot.

Enjoy your delicious homemade Naan Pizzas! They make a great quick meal or appetizer, and you can customize them with your favorite toppings.

Tempura Fish Tacos

Ingredients:

For the Tempura Fish:

- 1 lb (about 450g) white fish fillets (such as cod, tilapia, or haddock), cut into strips
- 1 cup all-purpose flour
- 1 teaspoon baking powder
- 1/2 teaspoon salt
- 1 cup ice-cold water
- Vegetable oil, for frying

For the Taco Assembly:

- 8 small flour or corn tortillas
- Shredded cabbage or lettuce
- Sliced avocado
- Sliced radishes
- Chopped cilantro
- Lime wedges
- Sriracha mayo or your favorite taco sauce

Instructions:

1. Prepare the Tempura Batter:
    - In a large bowl, whisk together the all-purpose flour, baking powder, and salt.
    - Gradually add the ice-cold water to the flour mixture, whisking until you have a smooth batter. The batter should be fairly thin.
2. Fry the Tempura Fish:
    - Heat vegetable oil in a deep skillet or pot to 350°F (175°C).
    - Dip the fish strips into the tempura batter, coating them evenly.
    - Carefully lower the battered fish strips into the hot oil, a few at a time, making sure not to overcrowd the skillet.

- Fry the fish strips for 3-4 minutes, or until they are golden brown and crispy.
- Remove the fried fish from the oil using a slotted spoon or tongs, and transfer them to a plate lined with paper towels to drain excess oil. Repeat until all the fish strips are cooked.

3. Assemble the Tacos:
    - Warm the tortillas in a dry skillet or microwave until soft and pliable.
    - Fill each tortilla with shredded cabbage or lettuce, sliced avocado, sliced radishes, and a few pieces of tempura fish.
    - Drizzle with sriracha mayo or your favorite taco sauce.
    - Garnish with chopped cilantro and serve with lime wedges on the side.
4. Serve:
    - Serve the Tempura Fish Tacos immediately, with extra lime wedges and taco sauce on the side if desired.
    - Enjoy the crispy, flavorful tempura fish wrapped in warm tortillas for a delicious meal!

These Tempura Fish Tacos are sure to be a hit with family and friends. They're perfect for a casual dinner or for entertaining guests!

Peruvian Lomo Saltado Fries

Ingredients:

For the Lomo Saltado:

- 1 lb (about 450g) beef steak (such as sirloin or ribeye), thinly sliced
- 2 tablespoons soy sauce
- 2 tablespoons red wine vinegar
- 2 tablespoons vegetable oil
- 1 onion, thinly sliced
- 1 bell pepper, thinly sliced
- 2 tomatoes, cut into wedges
- 3 cloves garlic, minced
- Salt and pepper, to taste
- A handful of fresh cilantro, chopped
- Cooked white rice, for serving

For the Fries:

- 4 large potatoes, cut into fries
- Vegetable oil, for frying
- Salt, to taste

Instructions:

1. Prepare the Lomo Saltado:
   - In a bowl, marinate the thinly sliced beef steak with soy sauce and red wine vinegar. Let it marinate for at least 15-20 minutes.
   - Heat vegetable oil in a large skillet or wok over high heat.
   - Add the marinated beef to the skillet and cook for 2-3 minutes until browned. Remove the beef from the skillet and set aside.
   - In the same skillet, add a little more oil if needed, then add the sliced onions and bell peppers. Cook for 2-3 minutes until slightly softened.
   - Add the minced garlic and cook for another minute.

- Return the cooked beef to the skillet and add the tomato wedges. Stir-fry everything together for another 2-3 minutes until the tomatoes are slightly softened.
- Season with salt and pepper to taste. Sprinkle chopped cilantro over the top and stir to combine.
- Remove from heat and keep warm.
2. Prepare the Fries:
    - Heat vegetable oil in a deep fryer or large pot to 350°F (175°C).
    - Fry the potato fries in batches until golden brown and crispy, about 5-7 minutes per batch. Drain on paper towels and season with salt while still hot.
3. Assemble the Lomo Saltado Fries:
    - Arrange the crispy fries on a serving platter.
    - Spoon the cooked Lomo Saltado mixture over the fries.
    - Serve immediately, with cooked white rice on the side if desired.
4. Serve:
    - Enjoy the delicious fusion of flavors in these Peruvian Lomo Saltado Fries!

This dish combines the best of both worlds: crispy fries with savory beef stir-fry, creating a flavorful and satisfying meal.

Bulgogi Beef Tacos

Ingredients:

For the Bulgogi Beef:

- 1 lb (about 450g) beef sirloin or ribeye, thinly sliced
- 1/4 cup soy sauce
- 2 tablespoons brown sugar
- 2 tablespoons sesame oil
- 2 cloves garlic, minced
- 1 tablespoon grated fresh ginger
- 2 green onions, thinly sliced
- 1 tablespoon sesame seeds
- 1 tablespoon rice vinegar
- 1 tablespoon vegetable oil, for cooking

For the Tacos:

- 8 small flour or corn tortillas
- Shredded lettuce or cabbage
- Thinly sliced cucumbers
- Thinly sliced radishes
- Kimchi (optional)
- Sriracha mayo or gochujang sauce (optional)
- Fresh cilantro leaves, for garnish
- Lime wedges, for serving

Instructions:

1. Marinate the Bulgogi Beef:
    - In a bowl, whisk together the soy sauce, brown sugar, sesame oil, minced garlic, grated ginger, sliced green onions, sesame seeds, and rice vinegar.
    - Add the thinly sliced beef to the marinade, making sure it's well coated. Cover and refrigerate for at least 30 minutes, or up to 2 hours.
2. Cook the Bulgogi Beef:

- Heat vegetable oil in a large skillet or wok over high heat.
- Add the marinated beef to the skillet in a single layer, reserving the marinade.
- Cook the beef for 2-3 minutes per side, or until browned and cooked through. Be careful not to overcrowd the skillet; you may need to cook the beef in batches.
- Remove the cooked beef from the skillet and set aside. Repeat with any remaining beef.

3. Assemble the Tacos:
   - Warm the tortillas in a dry skillet or microwave until soft and pliable.
   - Fill each tortilla with a portion of the cooked bulgogi beef.
   - Top with shredded lettuce or cabbage, thinly sliced cucumbers, thinly sliced radishes, and kimchi (if using).
   - Drizzle with sriracha mayo or gochujang sauce for extra flavor (if desired).
   - Garnish with fresh cilantro leaves and serve with lime wedges on the side.
4. Serve:
   - Serve the Bulgogi Beef Tacos immediately, with extra sriracha mayo or gochujang sauce on the side for dipping, if desired.
   - Enjoy the delicious fusion of Korean and Mexican flavors in these tasty tacos!

These Bulgogi Beef Tacos are perfect for a fun and flavorful meal that's sure to impress. Customize them with your favorite toppings and enjoy!

Shawarma Pizza

Ingredients:

For the Shawarma Chicken:

- 1 lb (about 450g) boneless, skinless chicken thighs, thinly sliced
- 2 tablespoons olive oil
- 2 cloves garlic, minced
- 1 teaspoon ground cumin
- 1 teaspoon ground paprika
- 1 teaspoon ground turmeric
- 1/2 teaspoon ground cinnamon
- Salt and pepper, to taste
- Juice of 1 lemon

For the Pizza:

- 1 pre-made pizza dough (store-bought or homemade)
- 1/2 cup tahini sauce
- 1 cup shredded mozzarella cheese
- 1/2 cup chopped tomatoes
- 1/4 cup sliced red onions
- 2 tablespoons chopped fresh parsley
- 1 tablespoon sesame seeds
- Lemon wedges, for serving

Instructions:

1. Prepare the Shawarma Chicken:
    - In a bowl, combine the olive oil, minced garlic, ground cumin, ground paprika, ground turmeric, ground cinnamon, salt, pepper, and lemon juice. Mix well to form a marinade.
    - Add the thinly sliced chicken thighs to the marinade, making sure they are well coated. Cover and refrigerate for at least 30 minutes, or up to 2 hours.
2. Cook the Shawarma Chicken:

- Heat a skillet over medium-high heat. Add the marinated chicken slices and cook for 5-6 minutes, stirring occasionally, until browned and cooked through. Remove from heat and set aside.

3. Assemble the Pizza:
   - Preheat your oven to the temperature recommended for your pizza dough.
   - Roll out the pizza dough on a lightly floured surface into your desired shape and thickness.
   - Transfer the rolled-out dough to a pizza pan or baking sheet lined with parchment paper.
   - Spread the tahini sauce evenly over the pizza dough, leaving a small border around the edges.
   - Sprinkle the cooked shawarma chicken evenly over the tahini sauce.
   - Top with shredded mozzarella cheese, chopped tomatoes, and sliced red onions.
   - Sprinkle chopped fresh parsley and sesame seeds over the top.
4. Bake the Pizza:
   - Place the assembled pizza in the preheated oven and bake according to the instructions for your pizza dough, usually 12-15 minutes, or until the crust is golden brown and the cheese is melted and bubbly.
5. Serve:
   - Remove the Shawarma Pizza from the oven and let it cool for a few minutes.
   - Slice the pizza into wedges and serve hot, with lemon wedges on the side for squeezing over the top if desired.
   - Enjoy the delicious fusion of flavors in this Shawarma Pizza!

This Shawarma Pizza is sure to be a hit with family and friends. It's perfect for a casual dinner or for entertaining guests!

Vietnamese Banh Xeo Tacos

Ingredients:

For the Banh Xeo Batter:

- 1 cup rice flour
- 1 cup coconut milk
- 3/4 cup water
- 1/2 teaspoon turmeric powder
- 1/2 teaspoon salt
- 2 green onions, thinly sliced
- 1/2 cup bean sprouts

For the Filling:

- 1 lb (about 450g) pork belly, thinly sliced
- 1/2 lb (about 225g) small shrimp, peeled and deveined
- 1 onion, thinly sliced
- 1 cup mung bean sprouts
- 1/2 cup sliced bell peppers
- 1/2 cup sliced carrots
- 2 cloves garlic, minced
- 2 tablespoons fish sauce
- 1 tablespoon sugar
- 1 tablespoon vegetable oil
- Lettuce leaves
- Fresh herbs (cilantro, mint, Thai basil)
- Lime wedges

For Serving:

- Hoisin sauce
- Sriracha or chili sauce
- Crushed peanuts

Instructions:

1. Prepare the Banh Xeo Batter:
   - In a large mixing bowl, whisk together rice flour, coconut milk, water, turmeric powder, and salt until smooth.
   - Stir in sliced green onions and bean sprouts. Let the batter rest for at least 30 minutes.
2. Cook the Filling:
   - Heat vegetable oil in a skillet over medium heat. Add minced garlic and sliced onions, cook until fragrant.
   - Add thinly sliced pork belly and cook until browned and cooked through.
   - Add shrimp, bell peppers, carrots, and mung bean sprouts. Cook until the shrimp turns pink.
   - Season with fish sauce and sugar. Stir well to combine. Remove from heat and set aside.
3. Cook the Banh Xeo:
   - Heat a non-stick skillet or crepe pan over medium-high heat. Brush with a little oil.
   - Pour a ladle of Banh Xeo batter into the skillet, swirling to coat the bottom evenly.
   - Cook until the edges are crispy and golden brown, and the bottom is cooked through, about 2-3 minutes.
   - Spoon some of the filling onto one half of the Banh Xeo, then fold it in half to cover the filling. Slide it onto a plate and keep warm.
   - Repeat with the remaining batter and filling.
4. Assemble the Tacos:
   - To assemble the Banh Xeo Tacos, place a piece of lettuce on each Banh Xeo shell.
   - Add a spoonful of the cooked filling on top of the lettuce.
   - Garnish with fresh herbs and a squeeze of lime juice.
5. Serve:
   - Serve the Banh Xeo Tacos with hoisin sauce, sriracha or chili sauce, and crushed peanuts on the side.
   - Enjoy the fusion flavors of these Vietnamese Banh Xeo Tacos!

These Banh Xeo Tacos offer a unique and delicious twist on traditional tacos, perfect for a fun and flavorful meal.

General Tso's Chicken Burrito

Ingredients:

For the General Tso's Chicken:

- 1 lb (about 450g) boneless, skinless chicken breasts, cut into bite-sized pieces
- 1/2 cup cornstarch
- 2 tablespoons vegetable oil
- 3 cloves garlic, minced
- 1 tablespoon grated ginger
- 1/2 cup soy sauce
- 1/4 cup hoisin sauce
- 3 tablespoons rice vinegar
- 2 tablespoons brown sugar
- 1 tablespoon cornstarch mixed with 2 tablespoons water
- 1 teaspoon sesame oil
- 1 teaspoon chili flakes (optional)
- Sesame seeds, for garnish (optional)
- Sliced green onions, for garnish (optional)

For the Burrito:

- Large flour tortillas
- Cooked white rice
- Black beans, drained and rinsed
- Shredded lettuce or cabbage
- Diced tomatoes
- Sliced avocado or guacamole
- Sour cream or Greek yogurt
- Sriracha or hot sauce (optional)

Instructions:

1. Prepare the General Tso's Chicken:
    - In a large bowl, toss the chicken pieces with cornstarch until well coated.
    - Heat vegetable oil in a large skillet or wok over medium-high heat.

- Add the cornstarch-coated chicken pieces to the skillet in a single layer. Cook until golden brown and cooked through, about 5-6 minutes per side. Remove the cooked chicken from the skillet and set aside.
- In the same skillet, add minced garlic and grated ginger. Cook for about 1 minute until fragrant.
- Add soy sauce, hoisin sauce, rice vinegar, brown sugar, and chili flakes (if using) to the skillet. Stir well to combine.
- Stir in the cornstarch-water mixture and cook until the sauce thickens, about 2-3 minutes.
- Return the cooked chicken to the skillet and toss to coat evenly in the sauce. Remove from heat and set aside.

2. Assemble the Burrito:
   - Warm the flour tortillas in a dry skillet or microwave until soft and pliable.
   - Place a generous scoop of cooked white rice in the center of each tortilla.
   - Top the rice with a spoonful of black beans, shredded lettuce or cabbage, diced tomatoes, sliced avocado or guacamole, and a scoop of General Tso's chicken.
   - Drizzle with sour cream or Greek yogurt and sriracha or hot sauce, if desired.

3. Fold the Burrito:
   - Fold the sides of the tortilla over the filling, then roll it up tightly from the bottom to enclose the filling.

4. Serve:
   - Serve the General Tso's Chicken Burritos immediately, whole or sliced in half.
   - Garnish with sesame seeds and sliced green onions, if desired.
   - Enjoy the delicious fusion flavors of these General Tso's Chicken Burritos!

These General Tso's Chicken Burritos offer a unique twist on traditional burritos, combining the bold flavors of Chinese-American cuisine with the convenience of a handheld wrap. They're perfect for a quick and satisfying meal!

Tandoori Chicken Tacos

Ingredients:

For the Tandoori Chicken:

- 1 lb (about 450g) boneless, skinless chicken thighs or breasts, cut into bite-sized pieces
- 1/2 cup plain yogurt
- 2 tablespoons tandoori masala spice blend
- 1 tablespoon lemon juice
- 2 cloves garlic, minced
- 1 tablespoon grated ginger
- 1 teaspoon ground cumin
- 1 teaspoon ground coriander
- 1/2 teaspoon turmeric powder
- Salt and pepper, to taste

For the Tacos:

- 8 small flour or corn tortillas
- Shredded lettuce or cabbage
- Sliced red onions
- Chopped tomatoes
- Chopped cilantro
- Lime wedges
- Greek yogurt or raita, for serving
- Mango salsa or chutney, for serving (optional)

Instructions:

1. Marinate the Tandoori Chicken:
    - In a bowl, combine plain yogurt, tandoori masala spice blend, lemon juice, minced garlic, grated ginger, ground cumin, ground coriander, turmeric powder, salt, and pepper.

- Add the chicken pieces to the marinade, making sure they are well coated. Cover and refrigerate for at least 1 hour, or overnight for best flavor.
2. Cook the Tandoori Chicken:
    - Preheat your grill or grill pan over medium-high heat.
    - Thread the marinated chicken pieces onto skewers if using.
    - Grill the chicken for 4-5 minutes per side, or until cooked through and charred in spots. Alternatively, you can cook the chicken in a skillet over medium-high heat for 6-8 minutes, stirring occasionally, until cooked through.
3. Assemble the Tacos:
    - Warm the tortillas in a dry skillet or microwave until soft and pliable.
    - Fill each tortilla with a portion of shredded lettuce or cabbage.
    - Top with cooked tandoori chicken pieces.
    - Add sliced red onions, chopped tomatoes, and chopped cilantro on top of the chicken.
    - Squeeze fresh lime juice over the tacos.
4. Serve:
    - Serve the Tandoori Chicken Tacos immediately, with Greek yogurt or raita on the side for drizzling or dipping.
    - Serve with mango salsa or chutney on the side for extra flavor, if desired.
    - Enjoy the delicious fusion flavors of these Tandoori Chicken Tacos!

These Tandoori Chicken Tacos are perfect for a fun and flavorful meal that combines the best of Indian and Mexican cuisines. Customize them with your favorite toppings and enjoy!

Korean Fried Chicken Waffle

Ingredients:

For the Korean Fried Chicken:

- 1 lb (about 450g) chicken wings or chicken drumsticks
- 1/2 cup all-purpose flour
- 1/2 cup cornstarch
- 1 teaspoon salt
- 1/2 teaspoon black pepper
- Vegetable oil, for frying
- 1/2 cup Korean fried chicken sauce (store-bought or homemade)
- Sesame seeds, for garnish
- Sliced green onions, for garnish

For the Waffles:

- 2 cups all-purpose flour
- 2 tablespoons granulated sugar
- 1 tablespoon baking powder
- 1/2 teaspoon salt
- 2 large eggs
- 1 3/4 cups milk
- 1/2 cup unsalted butter, melted
- Vegetable oil or non-stick spray, for greasing the waffle iron

Instructions:

1. Prepare the Korean Fried Chicken:
    - In a large bowl, mix together the all-purpose flour, cornstarch, salt, and black pepper.
    - Coat each piece of chicken in the flour mixture, shaking off any excess.
    - Heat vegetable oil in a deep fryer or large pot to 350°F (175°C).
    - Fry the coated chicken pieces in batches until golden brown and cooked through, about 8-10 minutes. Drain on a wire rack or paper towels.
    - In a separate bowl, toss the fried chicken pieces with Korean fried chicken sauce until evenly coated.

2. Make the Waffles:
   - Preheat your waffle iron according to the manufacturer's instructions.
   - In a large mixing bowl, whisk together the flour, sugar, baking powder, and salt.
   - In another bowl, whisk together the eggs, milk, and melted butter.
   - Pour the wet ingredients into the dry ingredients and stir until just combined. Be careful not to overmix; the batter should be slightly lumpy.
   - Grease the waffle iron with vegetable oil or non-stick spray.
   - Pour the waffle batter onto the hot waffle iron and cook according to the manufacturer's instructions until golden brown and crispy.
3. Assemble the Korean Fried Chicken Waffle:
   - Place a freshly cooked waffle on a plate.
   - Top the waffle with a generous portion of Korean fried chicken.
   - Sprinkle sesame seeds and sliced green onions on top for garnish.
4. Serve:
   - Serve the Korean Fried Chicken Waffle immediately, while the chicken is still hot and crispy, and the waffle is fresh and fluffy.
   - Enjoy the delicious fusion of flavors and textures in this unique dish!

This Korean Fried Chicken Waffle is perfect for brunch, lunch, or dinner. It's a delightful combination of sweet and savory flavors that will satisfy your cravings.

Thai Peanut Noodles Burrito

Ingredients:

For the Thai Peanut Noodles:

- 8 oz (about 225g) dried rice noodles
- 1/4 cup creamy peanut butter
- 2 tablespoons soy sauce
- 2 tablespoons rice vinegar
- 1 tablespoon sesame oil
- 1 tablespoon honey or brown sugar
- 2 cloves garlic, minced
- 1 tablespoon grated fresh ginger
- 1 tablespoon lime juice
- 1 teaspoon sriracha sauce (adjust to taste)
- 1/4 cup chopped cilantro
- 1/4 cup chopped peanuts
- Salt, to taste
- Water, as needed

For the Burrito:

- Large flour tortillas
- Cooked chicken, tofu, or shrimp (optional protein)
- Shredded lettuce or cabbage
- Shredded carrots
- Sliced bell peppers
- Thinly sliced cucumbers
- Sliced avocado or guacamole
- Fresh cilantro leaves
- Lime wedges

Instructions:

1. Prepare the Thai Peanut Noodles:

- Cook the rice noodles according to the package instructions until al dente. Drain and rinse under cold water to stop the cooking process. Set aside.
- In a small bowl, whisk together the creamy peanut butter, soy sauce, rice vinegar, sesame oil, honey or brown sugar, minced garlic, grated ginger, lime juice, and sriracha sauce until smooth. If the sauce is too thick, add water, a tablespoon at a time, until you reach your desired consistency.
- Toss the cooked noodles with the peanut sauce until evenly coated. Add chopped cilantro and chopped peanuts, and toss again. Season with salt to taste.

2. Assemble the Burrito:
    - Warm the flour tortillas in a dry skillet or microwave until soft and pliable.
    - Place a portion of the Thai peanut noodles in the center of each tortilla.
    - Add your choice of protein (if using), shredded lettuce or cabbage, shredded carrots, sliced bell peppers, thinly sliced cucumbers, and sliced avocado or guacamole on top of the noodles.
    - Garnish with fresh cilantro leaves and squeeze lime juice over the filling.
3. Fold the Burrito:
    - Fold the sides of the tortilla over the filling, then roll it up tightly from the bottom to enclose the filling.
4. Serve:
    - Serve the Thai Peanut Noodles Burrito immediately, whole or sliced in half.
    - Enjoy the unique fusion of flavors and textures in this delicious dish!

This Thai Peanut Noodles Burrito offers a creative twist on traditional burritos, combining the bold flavors of Thai cuisine with the convenience of a handheld wrap. Customize it with your favorite toppings and enjoy!

Gyro Fries

Ingredients:

For the Gyro Meat:

- 1 lb (about 450g) ground lamb or beef
- 1 small onion, finely chopped
- 2 cloves garlic, minced
- 1 teaspoon dried oregano
- 1 teaspoon dried thyme
- 1 teaspoon ground cumin
- 1 teaspoon ground coriander
- Salt and pepper, to taste

For the Tzatziki Sauce:

- 1 cup Greek yogurt
- 1/2 cucumber, grated and squeezed to remove excess moisture
- 2 cloves garlic, minced
- 1 tablespoon lemon juice
- 1 tablespoon chopped fresh dill (or 1 teaspoon dried dill)
- Salt and pepper, to taste

For the Fries:

- 1 lb (about 450g) frozen French fries
- Olive oil, for drizzling
- Salt, to taste

For Topping:

- Diced tomatoes
- Diced onions

- Crumbled feta cheese
- Chopped fresh parsley
- Kalamata olives, sliced (optional)

Instructions:

1. Prepare the Gyro Meat:
    - In a large mixing bowl, combine ground lamb or beef with chopped onion, minced garlic, dried oregano, dried thyme, ground cumin, ground coriander, salt, and pepper. Mix until well combined.
    - Heat a skillet over medium-high heat. Add the gyro meat mixture and cook, breaking it up with a spoon, until browned and cooked through. Remove from heat and set aside.
2. Make the Tzatziki Sauce:
    - In a bowl, combine Greek yogurt, grated cucumber, minced garlic, lemon juice, chopped fresh dill, salt, and pepper. Mix well. Cover and refrigerate until ready to use.
3. Prepare the Fries:
    - Preheat your oven according to the instructions on the package of frozen French fries.
    - Spread the frozen French fries in a single layer on a baking sheet. Drizzle with olive oil and sprinkle with salt, to taste.
    - Bake in the preheated oven until crispy and golden brown, following the instructions on the package.
4. Assemble the Gyro Fries:
    - Arrange the cooked French fries on a serving platter or individual plates.
    - Top the fries with the cooked gyro meat.
    - Drizzle the tzatziki sauce over the gyro meat.
    - Sprinkle diced tomatoes, diced onions, crumbled feta cheese, chopped fresh parsley, and sliced Kalamata olives (if using) over the top.
5. Serve:
    - Serve the Gyro Fries immediately, while the fries are hot and crispy.
    - Enjoy the delicious fusion of flavors in this loaded fries dish!

These Gyro Fries are perfect for a fun and flavorful meal or appetizer. They're sure to be a hit with family and friends!

Tikka Masala Burrito

Ingredients:

For the Chicken Tikka Masala:

- 1 lb (about 450g) boneless, skinless chicken breasts, cut into bite-sized pieces
- 1 cup plain yogurt
- 2 tablespoons tikka masala spice blend
- 2 tablespoons tomato paste
- 2 cloves garlic, minced
- 1 tablespoon grated fresh ginger
- 1 teaspoon ground cumin
- 1 teaspoon ground coriander
- 1/2 teaspoon turmeric powder
- 1/2 teaspoon cayenne pepper (adjust to taste)
- Salt and pepper, to taste
- 2 tablespoons vegetable oil
- 1 onion, finely chopped
- 1 can (14 oz) crushed tomatoes
- 1 cup heavy cream or coconut milk
- Fresh cilantro, chopped (for garnish)

For the Burrito:

- Large flour tortillas
- Cooked basmati rice
- Cooked lentils or chickpeas (optional)
- Sliced bell peppers
- Sliced onions
- Sliced cucumbers
- Shredded lettuce
- Sliced avocado or guacamole
- Lime wedges

Instructions:

1. Marinate the Chicken:
   - In a bowl, mix together plain yogurt, tikka masala spice blend, tomato paste, minced garlic, grated ginger, ground cumin, ground coriander, turmeric powder, cayenne pepper, salt, and pepper.
   - Add the chicken pieces to the marinade, making sure they are well coated. Cover and refrigerate for at least 1 hour, or overnight for best flavor.
2. Cook the Chicken Tikka Masala:
   - In a large skillet or pan, heat vegetable oil over medium-high heat.
   - Add chopped onion and cook until softened and translucent.
   - Add the marinated chicken along with any excess marinade to the skillet. Cook until the chicken is browned on all sides and cooked through.
   - Stir in the crushed tomatoes and heavy cream or coconut milk. Bring to a simmer and cook for an additional 5-7 minutes, until the sauce thickens slightly.
   - Adjust seasoning with salt and pepper, if needed. Remove from heat and set aside.
3. Assemble the Burrito:
   - Warm the flour tortillas in a dry skillet or microwave until soft and pliable.
   - Spread a portion of cooked basmati rice on each tortilla.
   - Top with a spoonful of the chicken tikka masala mixture.
   - Add cooked lentils or chickpeas (if using), sliced bell peppers, sliced onions, sliced cucumbers, shredded lettuce, and sliced avocado or guacamole on top of the chicken tikka masala.
   - Squeeze fresh lime juice over the filling.
4. Fold the Burrito:
   - Fold the sides of the tortilla over the filling, then roll it up tightly from the bottom to enclose the filling.
5. Serve:
   - Serve the Tikka Masala Burritos immediately, whole or sliced in half.
   - Garnish with chopped fresh cilantro.
   - Enjoy the delicious fusion flavors of these Tikka Masala Burritos!

These Tikka Masala Burritos offer a unique twist on traditional burritos, combining the rich and aromatic flavors of Indian cuisine with the convenience of a handheld wrap. Customize them with your favorite toppings and enjoy!

Ramen Tacos

Ingredients:

For the Ramen Noodles:

- 2 packs of instant ramen noodles (discard seasoning packets)
- Water for boiling

For the Taco Filling:

- 1 lb (about 450g) ground pork or chicken
- 2 cloves garlic, minced
- 1 tablespoon grated fresh ginger
- 2 tablespoons soy sauce
- 1 tablespoon hoisin sauce
- 1 tablespoon sesame oil
- 1 teaspoon sriracha sauce (adjust to taste)
- Salt and pepper to taste
- Vegetable oil for cooking

For the Toppings:

- Shredded cabbage or lettuce
- Thinly sliced green onions
- Chopped cilantro
- Sriracha mayo (mix sriracha sauce with mayonnaise)
- Lime wedges

For the Taco Shells:

- Small corn or flour tortillas

Instructions:

1. Prepare the Ramen Noodles:
   - Cook the instant ramen noodles according to the package instructions, but without adding the seasoning packets. Drain and set aside.
2. Cook the Taco Filling:
   - Heat a tablespoon of vegetable oil in a skillet over medium-high heat.
   - Add minced garlic and grated ginger, sauté until fragrant.
   - Add ground pork or chicken to the skillet, breaking it up with a spoon, and cook until browned and cooked through.
   - Stir in soy sauce, hoisin sauce, sesame oil, sriracha sauce, salt, and pepper. Cook for an additional 2-3 minutes. Remove from heat and set aside.
3. Assemble the Ramen Tacos:
   - Heat a small skillet over medium heat.
   - Place a tortilla in the skillet and heat on one side until warmed and slightly crispy.
   - Flip the tortilla and arrange a portion of cooked ramen noodles on one half of the tortilla.
   - Top the noodles with a generous spoonful of the cooked taco filling.
   - Add shredded cabbage or lettuce, thinly sliced green onions, and chopped cilantro on top.
   - Drizzle with sriracha mayo.
   - Squeeze fresh lime juice over the filling.
4. Fold and Serve:
   - Fold the tortilla in half, covering the filling.
   - Remove from the skillet and repeat with the remaining tortillas and filling.
   - Serve the Ramen Tacos immediately with lime wedges on the side.
5. Enjoy!
   - Enjoy the unique and flavorful fusion of ramen and tacos in this creative dish!

These Ramen Tacos are sure to be a hit with family and friends. Customize them with your favorite toppings and enjoy the delicious blend of flavors and textures!

Kimchi Fried Rice Burrito

Ingredients:

For the Kimchi Fried Rice:

- 2 cups cooked rice (preferably day-old)
- 1 cup kimchi, chopped
- 2 tablespoons kimchi juice (from the kimchi jar)
- 2 tablespoons soy sauce
- 1 tablespoon sesame oil
- 1 tablespoon vegetable oil
- 2 cloves garlic, minced
- 1 small onion, finely chopped
- 1 carrot, finely diced
- 1 cup cooked protein (such as diced chicken, pork, beef, tofu, or shrimp)
- 2 green onions, chopped
- Salt and pepper to taste

For the Burrito:

- Large flour tortillas
- Cooked rice or cooked quinoa
- Black beans, drained and rinsed
- Sliced avocado or guacamole
- Shredded lettuce
- Chopped fresh cilantro
- Sour cream or Greek yogurt (optional)
- Lime wedges

Instructions:

1. Prepare the Kimchi Fried Rice:
    - Heat vegetable oil in a large skillet or wok over medium-high heat.
    - Add minced garlic and chopped onion. Cook until softened and fragrant.
    - Add diced carrot and cook until slightly tender.

- Stir in chopped kimchi and cook for 2-3 minutes.
- Add cooked protein of your choice and cook until heated through.
- Add cooked rice to the skillet and break up any clumps. Stir in kimchi juice, soy sauce, and sesame oil. Cook, stirring frequently, until the rice is heated through and evenly coated with the sauce.
- Season with salt and pepper to taste. Stir in chopped green onions. Remove from heat and set aside.

2. Assemble the Burrito:
    - Warm the flour tortillas in a dry skillet or microwave until soft and pliable.
    - Spread a layer of cooked rice or cooked quinoa on each tortilla.
    - Spoon a generous portion of the kimchi fried rice onto the center of each tortilla.
    - Top with black beans, sliced avocado or guacamole, shredded lettuce, and chopped fresh cilantro.
    - If desired, add a dollop of sour cream or Greek yogurt on top.

3. Fold and Serve:
    - Fold the sides of the tortilla over the filling, then roll it up tightly from the bottom to enclose the filling.
    - Serve the Kimchi Fried Rice Burritos immediately, whole or sliced in half.
    - Serve with lime wedges on the side for squeezing over the burritos.

4. Enjoy!
    - Enjoy the delicious fusion flavors of these Kimchi Fried Rice Burritos!

These burritos are a fantastic way to enjoy the bold and tangy flavors of kimchi fried rice in a portable and convenient form. Customize them with your favorite toppings and enjoy!

Pad Thai Pizza

Ingredients:

For the Pizza Dough:

- 1 pound (about 450g) pizza dough, store-bought or homemade

For the Pad Thai Sauce:

- 1/4 cup soy sauce
- 3 tablespoons tamarind paste
- 2 tablespoons brown sugar
- 1 tablespoon fish sauce
- 1 tablespoon rice vinegar
- 1 teaspoon Sriracha sauce (adjust to taste)
- 2 cloves garlic, minced
- 1 teaspoon grated fresh ginger
- 1 tablespoon vegetable oil

For the Toppings:

- 1 cup cooked chicken, shrimp, or tofu, diced or shredded
- 1 cup bean sprouts
- 1/2 cup sliced red bell pepper
- 1/2 cup sliced green onions
- 1/4 cup chopped peanuts
- 1/4 cup chopped cilantro
- Lime wedges for serving

For Garnish (optional):

- Additional chopped peanuts
- Additional chopped cilantro
- Sriracha sauce

Instructions:

1. Preheat the Oven:
    - Preheat your oven to the temperature specified for your pizza dough (usually around 450°F or 230°C). Place a pizza stone or baking sheet in the oven to preheat as well.
2. Prepare the Pad Thai Sauce:
    - In a small saucepan, heat the vegetable oil over medium heat. Add the minced garlic and grated ginger, and cook for about 1 minute until fragrant.
    - Stir in the soy sauce, tamarind paste, brown sugar, fish sauce, rice vinegar, and Sriracha sauce. Bring the mixture to a simmer and cook for 2-3 minutes until the sauce thickens slightly. Remove from heat and set aside.
3. Roll Out the Pizza Dough:
    - On a lightly floured surface, roll out the pizza dough into a circle or rectangle, depending on your preference and the shape of your baking surface.
4. Assemble the Pizza:
    - Transfer the rolled-out pizza dough to a pizza peel or parchment paper if using a pizza stone, or directly onto a baking sheet if not using a pizza stone.
    - Spread a thin layer of the Pad Thai sauce over the pizza dough, leaving a small border around the edges.
    - Scatter the cooked chicken, shrimp, or tofu over the sauce, followed by the bean sprouts, sliced red bell pepper, and sliced green onions.
5. Bake the Pizza:
    - Transfer the assembled pizza to the preheated oven and bake according to the instructions for your pizza dough, usually 10-15 minutes, or until the crust is golden brown and the toppings are heated through.
6. Finish and Serve:
    - Remove the pizza from the oven and sprinkle chopped peanuts and chopped cilantro over the top.
    - Serve the Pad Thai Pizza hot, with lime wedges on the side for squeezing over the slices.
    - Optionally, garnish with additional chopped peanuts, chopped cilantro, and a drizzle of Sriracha sauce for extra flavor and spice.

Enjoy the unique and delicious flavors of Pad Thai in pizza form with this creative fusion recipe!

Falafel Tacos

Ingredients:

For the Falafel:

- 1 can (15 oz) chickpeas, drained and rinsed
- 1/2 cup chopped fresh parsley
- 1/2 cup chopped fresh cilantro
- 3 cloves garlic, minced
- 1 small onion, chopped
- 1 teaspoon ground cumin
- 1 teaspoon ground coriander
- 1/2 teaspoon baking powder
- 3 tablespoons all-purpose flour
- Salt and pepper to taste
- Vegetable oil for frying

For the Tacos:

- Small corn or flour tortillas
- Shredded lettuce
- Diced tomatoes
- Diced cucumbers
- Sliced red onions
- Tahini sauce or yogurt sauce
- Chopped fresh parsley or cilantro for garnish
- Lemon wedges for serving

Instructions:

1. Prepare the Falafel:
    - In a food processor, combine the chickpeas, chopped parsley, chopped cilantro, minced garlic, chopped onion, ground cumin, ground coriander, baking powder, flour, salt, and pepper.

- Pulse the mixture until well combined but still slightly chunky. You may need to scrape down the sides of the food processor a few times to ensure all ingredients are evenly mixed.
- Transfer the falafel mixture to a bowl, cover, and refrigerate for at least 30 minutes to allow the flavors to meld and the mixture to firm up.

2. Form and Cook the Falafel:
    - After chilling, remove the falafel mixture from the refrigerator.
    - Shape the falafel mixture into small patties, about 1 1/2 inches in diameter.
    - Heat vegetable oil in a skillet over medium heat. Once hot, add the falafel patties in batches and cook until golden brown and crispy on both sides, about 3-4 minutes per side. Transfer cooked falafel to a plate lined with paper towels to drain any excess oil.

3. Assemble the Tacos:
    - Warm the tortillas in a dry skillet or microwave until soft and pliable.
    - Place a few falafel patties in the center of each tortilla.
    - Top the falafel with shredded lettuce, diced tomatoes, diced cucumbers, and sliced red onions.
    - Drizzle with tahini sauce or yogurt sauce.

4. Garnish and Serve:
    - Sprinkle chopped fresh parsley or cilantro over the tacos for garnish.
    - Serve the Falafel Tacos immediately, accompanied by lemon wedges for squeezing over the tacos.

These Falafel Tacos offer a delightful fusion of flavors and textures, perfect for a unique and satisfying meal. Enjoy the delicious combination of Middle Eastern falafel and Mexican-inspired taco ingredients!

Bulgogi Burger

Ingredients:

For the Bulgogi Marinade:

- 1/4 cup soy sauce
- 2 tablespoons brown sugar
- 1 tablespoon sesame oil
- 2 cloves garlic, minced
- 1 teaspoon grated fresh ginger
- 2 tablespoons finely chopped green onions
- 1 tablespoon rice vinegar
- 1 tablespoon sesame seeds
- 1/4 teaspoon black pepper
- 1 lb (about 450g) ground beef (you can also use ground pork or chicken)

For the Burger Toppings:

- Burger buns
- Lettuce leaves
- Sliced tomatoes
- Sliced onions
- Sliced cheese (optional)
- Mayonnaise or Korean gochujang mayo (mix gochujang with mayo)
- Additional sesame seeds and chopped green onions for garnish

Instructions:

1. Prepare the Bulgogi Marinade:
    - In a bowl, whisk together soy sauce, brown sugar, sesame oil, minced garlic, grated ginger, chopped green onions, rice vinegar, sesame seeds, and black pepper until well combined.
2. Marinate the Ground Beef:
    - Place the ground beef in a large bowl and pour the bulgogi marinade over it.
    - Use your hands to thoroughly mix the marinade into the ground beef, ensuring it is evenly distributed.

- Cover the bowl with plastic wrap and refrigerate for at least 30 minutes to allow the flavors to meld.
3. Form the Burger Patties:
    - After marinating, divide the bulgogi-flavored ground beef mixture into equal portions and shape them into burger patties, ensuring they are slightly larger than the size of your burger buns to account for shrinkage during cooking.
4. Cook the Burger Patties:
    - Preheat your grill or skillet over medium-high heat.
    - Once hot, place the burger patties on the grill or skillet and cook for about 4-5 minutes per side, or until they reach your desired level of doneness.
    - If adding cheese, place a slice of cheese on top of each burger patty during the last minute of cooking and allow it to melt.
5. Assemble the Bulgogi Burgers:
    - Toast the burger buns lightly on the grill or in a toaster.
    - Place a lettuce leaf on the bottom half of each bun, followed by a burger patty.
    - Top the burger patties with sliced tomatoes, sliced onions, and any other desired toppings.
    - Spread a dollop of mayonnaise or Korean gochujang mayo on the top half of each bun.
    - Place the top half of the bun over the toppings to complete the burgers.
6. Garnish and Serve:
    - Sprinkle additional sesame seeds and chopped green onions over the assembled burgers for garnish.
    - Serve the Bulgogi Burgers immediately, accompanied by your favorite side dishes.

Enjoy the delicious fusion of Korean bulgogi flavors and classic burger goodness in these Bulgogi Burgers! They're sure to be a hit at your next barbecue or casual dinner.

Chicken Tikka Masala Pizza

Ingredients:

For the Pizza Dough:

- 1 pound (about 450g) pizza dough, store-bought or homemade

For the Chicken Tikka Masala:

- 1 lb (about 450g) boneless, skinless chicken breasts, cut into bite-sized pieces
- 1 cup plain yogurt
- 2 tablespoons tikka masala spice blend
- 2 tablespoons tomato paste
- 2 cloves garlic, minced
- 1 tablespoon grated fresh ginger
- 1 teaspoon ground cumin
- 1 teaspoon ground coriander
- 1/2 teaspoon turmeric powder
- 1/2 teaspoon cayenne pepper (adjust to taste)
- Salt and pepper to taste
- 2 tablespoons vegetable oil
- 1 onion, finely chopped
- 1 can (14 oz) crushed tomatoes
- 1/2 cup heavy cream or coconut milk
- Fresh cilantro, chopped (for garnish)

For the Pizza Toppings:

- Shredded mozzarella cheese
- Sliced red onions
- Sliced bell peppers
- Chopped fresh cilantro (for garnish)

Instructions:

1. Prepare the Chicken Tikka Masala:
    - In a bowl, mix together plain yogurt, tikka masala spice blend, tomato paste, minced garlic, grated ginger, ground cumin, ground coriander, turmeric powder, cayenne pepper, salt, and pepper.
    - Add the chicken pieces to the marinade, making sure they are well coated. Cover and refrigerate for at least 1 hour, or overnight for best flavor.
    - In a large skillet or pan, heat vegetable oil over medium-high heat.
    - Add chopped onion and cook until softened and translucent.
    - Add the marinated chicken along with any excess marinade to the skillet. Cook until the chicken is browned on all sides and cooked through.
    - Stir in the crushed tomatoes and heavy cream or coconut milk. Bring to a simmer and cook for an additional 5-7 minutes, until the sauce thickens slightly.
    - Adjust seasoning with salt and pepper, if needed. Remove from heat and set aside.
2. Prepare the Pizza:
    - Preheat your oven according to the instructions for your pizza dough (usually around 450°F or 230°C). Place a pizza stone or baking sheet in the oven to preheat as well.
    - Roll out the pizza dough on a floured surface into the desired shape and thickness.
    - Transfer the rolled-out dough to a pizza peel or parchment paper for easy transfer to the oven.
    - Spread a layer of the chicken tikka masala sauce over the pizza dough, leaving a small border around the edges.
    - Sprinkle shredded mozzarella cheese over the sauce.
    - Add sliced red onions and bell peppers on top of the cheese.
    - Bake the pizza in the preheated oven for 12-15 minutes, or until the crust is golden brown and the cheese is melted and bubbly.
    - Remove the pizza from the oven and garnish with chopped fresh cilantro.
    - Slice and serve hot. Enjoy your Chicken Tikka Masala Pizza!

This pizza combines the bold flavors of chicken tikka masala with the comfort of a pizza, making it a delicious and satisfying meal for any occasion.

Tempura Shrimp Po' Boy

Ingredients:

For the Tempura Shrimp:

- 1 lb (about 450g) large shrimp, peeled and deveined
- 1 cup all-purpose flour
- 1/2 cup cornstarch
- 1 teaspoon baking powder
- 1/2 teaspoon salt
- 1 cup cold water
- Vegetable oil for frying

For the Sandwich:

- French bread or baguette, cut into sandwich-sized pieces
- Shredded lettuce
- Sliced tomatoes
- Sliced pickles
- Mayonnaise or remoulade sauce
- Lemon wedges for serving

Instructions:

1. Prepare the Tempura Shrimp:
    - In a large bowl, whisk together the all-purpose flour, cornstarch, baking powder, and salt.
    - Gradually add the cold water to the dry ingredients, whisking until smooth and well combined.
    - Heat vegetable oil in a deep fryer or large pot to 350°F (180°C).
    - Dip each shrimp into the tempura batter, allowing any excess batter to drip off.
    - Carefully place the battered shrimp into the hot oil and fry in batches for 2-3 minutes, or until golden brown and crispy.

- Remove the fried shrimp from the oil using a slotted spoon and transfer them to a plate lined with paper towels to drain any excess oil. Keep warm while you assemble the sandwiches.
2. Assemble the Sandwiches:
    - Slice the French bread or baguette pieces horizontally, without cutting all the way through, to create a pocket for the fillings.
    - Spread mayonnaise or remoulade sauce on the inside of each bread piece.
    - Layer shredded lettuce, sliced tomatoes, and sliced pickles on the bottom half of each sandwich.
    - Place the crispy tempura shrimp on top of the vegetables.
    - Close the sandwiches with the top halves of the bread.
3. Serve:
    - Serve the Tempura Shrimp Po' Boys immediately, accompanied by lemon wedges for squeezing over the sandwiches.
    - Optionally, serve with additional remoulade sauce or hot sauce on the side for dipping.

Enjoy the crispy and flavorful Tempura Shrimp Po' Boys as a delicious meal, perfect for lunch or dinner!

Sushi Pizza

Ingredients:

For the Sushi Rice Base:

- 2 cups sushi rice
- 2 1/2 cups water
- 1/3 cup rice vinegar
- 3 tablespoons sugar
- 1 teaspoon salt

For the Toppings:

- Sushi-grade fish (such as tuna, salmon, or yellowtail), thinly sliced
- Avocado, thinly sliced
- Cucumber, thinly sliced
- Sesame seeds
- Nori (seaweed sheets), cut into thin strips
- Spicy mayo (mix mayonnaise with Sriracha sauce)
- Soy sauce for drizzling (optional)
- Wasabi and pickled ginger for serving (optional)

Instructions:

1. Prepare the Sushi Rice Base:
    - Rinse the sushi rice under cold water until the water runs clear. Drain well.
    - In a rice cooker or pot, combine the rinsed sushi rice and water. Cook according to the rice cooker's instructions or bring to a boil, then reduce the heat to low, cover, and simmer for 18-20 minutes, or until the rice is cooked and tender.
    - In a small saucepan, combine the rice vinegar, sugar, and salt. Heat over low heat until the sugar and salt are dissolved, stirring occasionally.
    - Transfer the cooked rice to a large bowl and gently fold in the seasoned rice vinegar mixture until well combined. Allow the rice to cool to room temperature.

2. Assemble the Sushi Pizza:
    - Preheat your oven to 375°F (190°C).
    - Line a baking sheet or pizza pan with parchment paper.
    - Spread the cooled sushi rice evenly onto the prepared baking sheet or pizza pan, pressing down gently to compact the rice into a thin, even layer. You can shape it into a round or rectangular shape, similar to a pizza crust.
    - Bake the sushi rice crust in the preheated oven for 10-12 minutes, or until the edges are slightly golden and crispy.
    - Remove the sushi rice crust from the oven and let it cool slightly.
3. Add the Toppings:
    - Arrange the thinly sliced fish, avocado, and cucumber over the baked sushi rice crust.
    - Drizzle the top with spicy mayo and sprinkle sesame seeds and nori strips over the toppings.
4. Serve:
    - Slice the sushi pizza into wedges or squares.
    - Serve immediately, with soy sauce, wasabi, and pickled ginger on the side for dipping, if desired.

Enjoy your homemade Sushi Pizza as a fun and flavorful twist on traditional sushi and pizza!

BBQ Pork Belly Tacos

Ingredients:

For the BBQ Pork Belly:

- 1 lb (about 450g) pork belly, skin removed and cut into small cubes
- 1/2 cup barbecue sauce (store-bought or homemade)
- 2 cloves garlic, minced
- 1 tablespoon soy sauce
- 1 tablespoon brown sugar
- 1 teaspoon smoked paprika
- 1/2 teaspoon chili powder
- Salt and pepper to taste
- Vegetable oil for cooking

For the Tacos:

- Small corn or flour tortillas
- Shredded cabbage or lettuce
- Diced tomatoes
- Sliced red onions
- Chopped cilantro
- Lime wedges for serving

Instructions:

1. Marinate the Pork Belly:
   - In a bowl, combine the barbecue sauce, minced garlic, soy sauce, brown sugar, smoked paprika, chili powder, salt, and pepper.
   - Add the cubed pork belly to the marinade and toss until well coated. Cover and refrigerate for at least 1 hour, or overnight for best flavor.
2. Cook the Pork Belly:
   - Heat a tablespoon of vegetable oil in a skillet or frying pan over medium-high heat.
   - Add the marinated pork belly cubes to the skillet in a single layer, making sure not to overcrowd the pan.

- Cook the pork belly for 3-4 minutes on each side, or until browned and caramelized.
- Pour any remaining marinade into the skillet and cook for an additional 2-3 minutes, or until the sauce thickens and coats the pork belly.

3. Assemble the Tacos:
    - Warm the tortillas in a dry skillet or microwave until soft and pliable.
    - Place a spoonful of shredded cabbage or lettuce on each tortilla.
    - Top with a few pieces of the cooked pork belly.
    - Garnish with diced tomatoes, sliced red onions, and chopped cilantro.
    - Squeeze a wedge of lime over each taco for a burst of freshness.
4. Serve:
    - Serve the BBQ Pork Belly Tacos immediately, accompanied by extra lime wedges on the side.
    - Optionally, serve with additional barbecue sauce for dipping or drizzling.

Enjoy the flavorful and satisfying BBQ Pork Belly Tacos as a delicious meal for any occasion!

Peruvian Chicken Empanadas

Ingredients:

- For the Dough:
    - 2 cups all-purpose flour
    - 1 teaspoon salt
    - ⅓ cup cold unsalted butter, cut into cubes
    - 1 large egg
    - ¼ cup cold water
- For the Filling:
    - 2 cups cooked chicken, shredded
    - 1 small onion, finely chopped
    - 1 red bell pepper, finely chopped
    - 2 cloves garlic, minced
    - 1 teaspoon ground cumin
    - 1 teaspoon paprika
    - ½ teaspoon dried oregano
    - Salt and pepper to taste
    - 2 tablespoons olive oil
    - ½ cup frozen corn kernels
    - ½ cup frozen peas
    - ½ cup shredded mozzarella cheese
    - 2 tablespoons chopped fresh cilantro (optional)
    - Egg wash (1 egg beaten with 1 tablespoon water), for brushing

Instructions:

1. Prepare the Dough:
    - In a large mixing bowl, combine the flour and salt. Cut in the cold butter using a pastry cutter or fork until the mixture resembles coarse crumbs.
    - In a small bowl, whisk together the egg and cold water. Gradually add the egg mixture to the flour mixture, stirring until a dough forms. If the dough is too dry, add a little more water, one tablespoon at a time.
    - Turn the dough out onto a lightly floured surface and knead gently until smooth. Wrap the dough in plastic wrap and refrigerate for at least 30 minutes.
2. Make the Filling:

- In a large skillet, heat the olive oil over medium heat. Add the onion and red bell pepper and cook until softened, about 5 minutes.
- Add the minced garlic, ground cumin, paprika, dried oregano, salt, and pepper. Cook for another 2 minutes, stirring frequently.
- Stir in the shredded chicken, frozen corn, and peas. Cook for an additional 5 minutes, then remove from heat. Allow the filling to cool slightly before assembling the empanadas.

3. Assemble the Empanadas:
    - Preheat your oven to 375°F (190°C). Line a baking sheet with parchment paper.
    - Roll out the chilled dough on a lightly floured surface to about ⅛ inch thickness. Use a round cutter or a small plate to cut out circles of dough, about 5-6 inches in diameter.
    - Place a spoonful of the chicken filling in the center of each dough circle. Sprinkle with shredded mozzarella cheese and chopped cilantro, if desired.
    - Fold the dough over the filling to create a half-moon shape. Use a fork to crimp the edges of the empanadas to seal them shut.
    - Place the assembled empanadas on the prepared baking sheet. Brush the tops with egg wash.
4. Bake the Empanadas:
    - Bake in the preheated oven for 20-25 minutes, or until the empanadas are golden brown and crispy.
    - Remove from the oven and let cool for a few minutes before serving.

These Peruvian Chicken Empanadas are delicious served hot or at room temperature. Enjoy them as a snack, appetizer, or even a main course!

Shawarma Burrito

Ingredients:

- For the Shawarma Chicken:
    - 1 pound boneless, skinless chicken thighs, thinly sliced
    - 2 cloves garlic, minced
    - 2 tablespoons lemon juice
    - 2 tablespoons olive oil
    - 1 teaspoon ground cumin
    - 1 teaspoon paprika
    - ½ teaspoon ground turmeric
    - ½ teaspoon ground coriander
    - Salt and pepper to taste
    - 2 tablespoons plain yogurt (optional, for added tenderness)
- For the Burrito:
    - Large flour tortillas
    - Hummus
    - Tabbouleh or chopped parsley
    - Sliced tomatoes
    - Sliced cucumbers
    - Sliced red onions
    - Pickled turnips or cucumbers
    - Tahini sauce or garlic sauce
    - Chili sauce (optional, for heat)

Instructions:

1. Marinate the Chicken:
    - In a bowl, combine the minced garlic, lemon juice, olive oil, ground cumin, paprika, turmeric, coriander, salt, and pepper. If using, add the plain yogurt.
    - Add the sliced chicken thighs to the marinade and toss until well coated. Cover the bowl and refrigerate for at least 1 hour, or preferably overnight, to allow the flavors to meld.
2. Cook the Chicken:
    - Heat a skillet over medium-high heat. Once hot, add the marinated chicken thighs along with any excess marinade.

- Cook the chicken, stirring occasionally, until it is cooked through and nicely browned, about 6-8 minutes. Remove from heat and set aside.

3. Assemble the Burrito:
    - Warm the flour tortillas in a dry skillet or microwave.
    - Spread a generous layer of hummus across the center of each tortilla.
    - Layer the cooked shawarma chicken on top of the hummus.
    - Add sliced tomatoes, cucumbers, red onions, pickled turnips or cucumbers, and tabbouleh or chopped parsley on top of the chicken.
    - Drizzle with tahini sauce or garlic sauce, and add chili sauce if desired.

4. Roll the Burrito:
    - Fold the sides of the tortilla over the filling.
    - Starting from the bottom, tightly roll the tortilla up to form a burrito shape.
    - Optionally, you can wrap the burrito in parchment paper or aluminum foil to help hold its shape and keep it together.

5. Serve:
    - Slice the shawarma burrito in half diagonally, if desired, and serve immediately.
    - Enjoy your delicious Shawarma Burrito as a satisfying meal on the go or as part of a Middle Eastern-inspired feast!

Feel free to customize your Shawarma Burrito with additional toppings or sauces according to your taste preferences.

Thai Basil Chicken Waffle

Ingredients:

- For the Thai Basil Chicken:
    - 1 lb boneless, skinless chicken breasts or thighs, thinly sliced
    - 2 tablespoons oyster sauce
    - 2 tablespoons soy sauce
    - 1 tablespoon fish sauce
    - 1 tablespoon brown sugar
    - 2 cloves garlic, minced
    - 1 shallot, finely chopped
    - 1 red chili pepper, thinly sliced (adjust amount to taste)
    - 1 cup fresh Thai basil leaves, loosely packed
    - 2 tablespoons vegetable oil for cooking
- For the Waffles:
    - 2 cups all-purpose flour
    - 2 teaspoons baking powder
    - 1 tablespoon sugar
    - ½ teaspoon salt
    - 1¾ cups milk
    - 2 large eggs
    - ½ cup unsalted butter, melted
    - Cooking spray or extra butter for greasing the waffle iron

Instructions:

1. Prepare the Thai Basil Chicken:
    - In a bowl, mix together the oyster sauce, soy sauce, fish sauce, and brown sugar until well combined. Set aside.
    - Heat the vegetable oil in a large skillet or wok over medium-high heat. Add the minced garlic, chopped shallot, and sliced chili pepper. Stir-fry for 1-2 minutes until fragrant.
    - Add the sliced chicken to the skillet and cook until it is no longer pink, about 5-6 minutes.
    - Pour the sauce mixture over the chicken and toss until the chicken is evenly coated. Cook for another 2-3 minutes, allowing the sauce to thicken slightly.

- Remove the skillet from heat and stir in the fresh Thai basil leaves. Set aside while you make the waffles.
2. Make the Waffles:
    - Preheat your waffle iron according to manufacturer's instructions.
    - In a large mixing bowl, whisk together the flour, baking powder, sugar, and salt.
    - In another bowl, whisk together the milk, eggs, and melted butter until well combined.
    - Pour the wet ingredients into the dry ingredients and stir until just combined. Be careful not to overmix; a few lumps are okay.
    - Lightly grease the waffle iron with cooking spray or brush with melted butter.
    - Pour the batter onto the preheated waffle iron and cook according to the manufacturer's instructions, until the waffles are golden brown and crispy.
3. Assemble the Thai Basil Chicken Waffles:
    - Place a cooked waffle on a plate or serving platter.
    - Spoon a generous portion of the Thai basil chicken over the waffle.
    - Garnish with additional fresh Thai basil leaves and sliced chili peppers, if desired.
    - Serve immediately and enjoy the delicious fusion of flavors!

These Thai Basil Chicken Waffles are a delightful blend of sweet, savory, and spicy flavors. They make a unique and satisfying meal that's perfect for brunch, lunch, or dinner.

Korean BBQ Pizza

Ingredients:

- For the Pizza Dough:
    - 1 pound pizza dough (store-bought or homemade)
    - Cornmeal or flour, for dusting
- For the Korean BBQ Sauce:
    - ⅓ cup soy sauce
    - 2 tablespoons brown sugar
    - 2 tablespoons honey
    - 2 tablespoons rice vinegar
    - 2 cloves garlic, minced
    - 1 tablespoon sesame oil
    - 1 teaspoon grated ginger
    - 1 tablespoon Korean chili paste (gochujang), adjust to taste
    - 1 tablespoon cornstarch mixed with 2 tablespoons water (optional, for thickening)
- For the Toppings:
    - 1 cup cooked and shredded chicken or pork (you can use leftover Korean barbecue meat)
    - 1 cup shredded mozzarella cheese
    - ½ cup shredded sharp cheddar cheese
    - ½ cup thinly sliced red onion
    - ½ cup thinly sliced bell peppers (any color)
    - 2 green onions, thinly sliced
    - Sesame seeds, for garnish
    - Chopped fresh cilantro or parsley, for garnish

Instructions:

1. Prepare the Korean BBQ Sauce:
    - In a small saucepan, combine the soy sauce, brown sugar, honey, rice vinegar, minced garlic, sesame oil, grated ginger, and Korean chili paste (gochujang).
    - Bring the mixture to a simmer over medium heat, stirring occasionally, and let it cook for about 5-7 minutes until slightly thickened. If you prefer a

thicker sauce, you can add the cornstarch-water mixture and cook until further thickened. Remove from heat and set aside to cool.

2. Preheat the Oven:
    - Preheat your oven to the temperature specified on the pizza dough package or to 450°F (230°C). If you have a pizza stone, place it in the oven to preheat as well.
3. Prepare the Pizza Dough:
    - On a lightly floured surface, roll out the pizza dough into your desired shape and thickness. If using a pizza stone, sprinkle cornmeal on a pizza peel or the back of a baking sheet.
4. Assemble the Pizza:
    - Spread a layer of the Korean BBQ sauce evenly over the rolled-out pizza dough, leaving a small border around the edges.
    - Sprinkle the shredded chicken or pork evenly over the sauce.
    - Scatter the sliced red onion and bell peppers over the meat.
    - Top with a combination of shredded mozzarella and cheddar cheese.
5. Bake the Pizza:
    - Carefully transfer the assembled pizza to the preheated pizza stone or baking sheet.
    - Bake in the preheated oven for 12-15 minutes, or until the crust is golden brown and the cheese is melted and bubbly.
6. Finish and Serve:
    - Once the pizza is out of the oven, sprinkle with sliced green onions, sesame seeds, and chopped cilantro or parsley for added flavor and freshness.
    - Slice the pizza and serve hot. Enjoy the unique fusion of Korean barbecue flavors with the classic comfort of pizza!

This Korean BBQ Pizza makes a fantastic meal for gatherings, parties, or simply when you're craving something different and delicious. Feel free to customize the toppings to suit your taste preferences.

Banh Mi Burger

Ingredients:

- For the Burger Patties:
    - 1 pound ground beef or pork
    - 2 cloves garlic, minced
    - 2 green onions, finely chopped
    - 1 tablespoon fish sauce
    - 1 tablespoon soy sauce
    - 1 tablespoon brown sugar
    - 1 teaspoon ground black pepper
    - 1 teaspoon sesame oil
    - 1 teaspoon grated ginger
- For the Pickled Vegetables:
    - 1 medium carrot, julienned
    - ½ English cucumber, thinly sliced
    - ½ cup rice vinegar
    - 2 tablespoons sugar
    - 1 teaspoon salt
- For the Sriracha Mayo:
    - ½ cup mayonnaise
    - 2 tablespoons Sriracha sauce (adjust to taste)
- Additional Ingredients:
    - Burger buns or crusty rolls
    - Fresh cilantro sprigs
    - Sliced jalapeños
    - Thinly sliced red onion
    - Sliced cucumber
    - Thinly sliced radishes
    - Thinly sliced green onions

Instructions:

1. Prepare the Pickled Vegetables:
    - In a small saucepan, combine the rice vinegar, sugar, and salt. Heat over medium heat, stirring until the sugar and salt dissolve.

- Place the julienned carrots and sliced cucumber in a heatproof jar or bowl. Pour the hot vinegar mixture over the vegetables, ensuring they are completely submerged. Let cool to room temperature, then cover and refrigerate for at least 1 hour, or preferably overnight.
2. Make the Sriracha Mayo:
    - In a small bowl, mix together the mayonnaise and Sriracha sauce until well combined. Adjust the amount of Sriracha to taste. Cover and refrigerate until ready to use.
3. Prepare the Burger Patties:
    - In a large mixing bowl, combine the ground meat, minced garlic, finely chopped green onions, fish sauce, soy sauce, brown sugar, ground black pepper, sesame oil, and grated ginger. Mix until all ingredients are evenly distributed.
    - Divide the mixture into equal portions and shape them into burger patties. Make an indentation in the center of each patty with your thumb to prevent them from puffing up during cooking.
4. Cook the Burger Patties:
    - Heat a grill or skillet over medium-high heat. Once hot, cook the burger patties for 4-5 minutes per side, or until cooked to your desired level of doneness.
5. Assemble the Banh Mi Burgers:
    - Toast the burger buns or crusty rolls on the grill or in a toaster until lightly golden.
    - Spread a generous amount of Sriracha mayo on the bottom half of each bun.
    - Place a cooked burger patty on top of the mayo.
    - Layer with pickled vegetables, sliced jalapeños, red onion, cucumber, radishes, green onions, and fresh cilantro sprigs.
    - Top with the other half of the bun.
6. Serve:
    - Serve the Banh Mi Burgers immediately, accompanied by additional Sriracha mayo and pickled vegetables on the side if desired.
    - Enjoy the fusion of bold flavors and textures in each bite!

These Banh Mi Burgers are perfect for a casual weeknight dinner or a weekend barbecue with friends and family. Customize the toppings to suit your taste preferences, and don't be afraid to get creative!

General Tso's Chicken Tacos

Ingredients:

- For the General Tso's Chicken:
    - 1 pound boneless, skinless chicken thighs, cut into bite-sized pieces
    - ½ cup cornstarch
    - Salt and pepper, to taste
    - 2 tablespoons vegetable oil
    - 2 cloves garlic, minced
    - 1 teaspoon grated ginger
    - ⅓ cup soy sauce
    - ⅓ cup hoisin sauce
    - 2 tablespoons rice vinegar
    - 2 tablespoons brown sugar
    - 1 tablespoon cornstarch mixed with 2 tablespoons water (slurry)
    - Sliced green onions, for garnish
    - Sesame seeds, for garnish
- For the Taco Assembly:
    - Small flour or corn tortillas
    - Shredded lettuce or cabbage
    - Sliced red bell peppers
    - Sliced green onions
    - Thinly sliced red cabbage
    - Sriracha mayo or spicy mayo, for drizzling
    - Fresh cilantro, for garnish
    - Lime wedges, for serving

Instructions:

1. Prepare the General Tso's Chicken:
    - In a bowl, season the chicken pieces with salt and pepper, then toss them in cornstarch until evenly coated.
    - Heat the vegetable oil in a large skillet or wok over medium-high heat. Add the coated chicken pieces and cook until golden brown and crispy, about 5-6 minutes per side. Remove the chicken from the skillet and set aside.
2. Make the General Tso's Sauce:

- In the same skillet, add a little more oil if needed. Add the minced garlic and grated ginger, and sauté for about 1 minute until fragrant.
- Stir in the soy sauce, hoisin sauce, rice vinegar, and brown sugar. Cook for another 2-3 minutes, stirring occasionally.
- Add the cornstarch slurry to the sauce and stir well. Cook for an additional minute until the sauce thickens.
- Return the cooked chicken to the skillet and toss until the chicken is coated evenly with the sauce. Cook for another minute to heat through.

3. Assemble the Tacos:
    - Warm the tortillas in a dry skillet or microwave until soft and pliable.
    - Place a portion of shredded lettuce or cabbage on each tortilla.
    - Top with the General Tso's chicken, sliced red bell peppers, green onions, and thinly sliced red cabbage.
    - Drizzle with Sriracha mayo or spicy mayo for an extra kick.
    - Garnish with fresh cilantro and sesame seeds.
4. Serve:
    - Serve the General Tso's Chicken Tacos immediately, accompanied by lime wedges for squeezing over the tacos.
    - Enjoy the flavorful fusion of Chinese-American and Mexican cuisines in each bite!

These General Tso's Chicken Tacos are perfect for a fun and creative meal that will surely impress your family and friends. Feel free to customize the toppings according to your preferences, and don't forget to serve with extra napkins!

Teriyaki Salmon Poke Bowl

Ingredients:

- For the Teriyaki Salmon:
    - 1 pound fresh salmon fillet, skin removed, cut into bite-sized cubes
    - ¼ cup soy sauce
    - 2 tablespoons mirin
    - 1 tablespoon honey
    - 1 tablespoon sesame oil
    - 2 cloves garlic, minced
    - 1 teaspoon grated ginger
    - 1 tablespoon cornstarch mixed with 2 tablespoons water (slurry)
    - Sesame seeds, for garnish
    - Sliced green onions, for garnish
- For the Poke Bowl:
    - Cooked sushi rice or brown rice
    - Mixed salad greens or spinach
    - Sliced cucumber
    - Sliced avocado
    - Shredded carrots
    - Edamame beans, cooked and shelled
    - Pickled ginger
    - Nori strips or seaweed salad
    - Sriracha mayo or spicy mayo, for drizzling
    - Soy sauce or additional teriyaki sauce, for drizzling
    - Lime wedges, for serving

Instructions:

1. Prepare the Teriyaki Salmon:
    - In a bowl, combine the soy sauce, mirin, honey, sesame oil, minced garlic, and grated ginger to make the teriyaki sauce.
    - Place the salmon cubes in a shallow dish or resealable plastic bag. Pour half of the teriyaki sauce over the salmon and toss to coat. Reserve the remaining sauce for drizzling over the poke bowl.
    - Marinate the salmon in the refrigerator for at least 30 minutes, or up to 1 hour.

2. Cook the Salmon:
   - Heat a non-stick skillet or grill pan over medium-high heat. Once hot, add the marinated salmon cubes to the pan, reserving any excess marinade.
   - Cook the salmon for 2-3 minutes on each side, or until it is cooked through and nicely caramelized. Use a brush to baste the salmon with the remaining teriyaki sauce while cooking.
   - Once cooked, transfer the salmon to a plate and set aside.
3. Assemble the Poke Bowl:
   - Start by placing a serving of cooked sushi rice or brown rice in the bottom of each bowl.
   - Arrange a variety of mixed salad greens or spinach, sliced cucumber, sliced avocado, shredded carrots, and edamame beans around the rice.
   - Top the bowl with the cooked teriyaki salmon cubes.
   - Garnish with pickled ginger, nori strips or seaweed salad, sesame seeds, and sliced green onions.
   - Drizzle with Sriracha mayo or spicy mayo, and soy sauce or additional teriyaki sauce for extra flavor.
4. Serve:
   - Serve the Teriyaki Salmon Poke Bowls immediately, accompanied by lime wedges for squeezing over the bowl.
   - Enjoy the delicious combination of flavors and textures in each bite!

These Teriyaki Salmon Poke Bowls are perfect for a light and nutritious meal that's bursting with flavor. Feel free to customize the toppings according to your preferences, and enjoy the fresh and vibrant taste of this Japanese-inspired dish!

Naan Tacos

Ingredients:

- For the Naan Bread:
    - Store-bought or homemade naan bread
- For the Taco Fillings:
    - Cooked protein of your choice (such as grilled chicken, beef, shrimp, or tofu)
    - Black beans, drained and rinsed
    - Sautéed bell peppers and onions
    - Shredded lettuce or cabbage
    - Diced tomatoes
    - Sliced avocado or guacamole
    - Shredded cheese (such as cheddar, Monterey Jack, or Mexican blend)
    - Sliced jalapeños (optional, for heat)
    - Fresh cilantro, chopped
    - Lime wedges, for serving
- For the Sauce:
    - ½ cup Greek yogurt or sour cream
    - 1 tablespoon lime juice
    - 1 teaspoon chili powder
    - ½ teaspoon ground cumin
    - Salt and pepper, to taste

Instructions:

1. Prepare the Naan Bread:
    - Warm the naan bread according to the package instructions or heat it in a skillet over medium heat for a few minutes on each side until warmed through and lightly toasted. Set aside.
2. Prepare the Taco Fillings:
    - Cook your choice of protein (chicken, beef, shrimp, or tofu) using your preferred method (grilling, sautéing, etc.). Season with taco seasoning for extra flavor if desired.
    - Warm the black beans in a small saucepan over medium heat until heated through.

- Sauté bell peppers and onions in a skillet with a little oil until they are tender and caramelized.
3. Prepare the Sauce:
    - In a small bowl, whisk together the Greek yogurt or sour cream, lime juice, chili powder, ground cumin, salt, and pepper until smooth. Adjust seasoning to taste.
4. Assemble the Naan Tacos:
    - Lay out the warmed naan bread on a flat surface.
    - Spread a layer of the prepared sauce over each naan bread.
    - Top with your choice of cooked protein, black beans, sautéed bell peppers and onions, shredded lettuce or cabbage, diced tomatoes, sliced avocado or guacamole, shredded cheese, sliced jalapeños (if using), and fresh cilantro.
5. Serve:
    - Serve the Naan Tacos immediately, accompanied by lime wedges for squeezing over the tacos.
    - Enjoy the delicious fusion of Indian and Mexican flavors in each bite!

These Naan Tacos are versatile and customizable, making them perfect for a casual dinner or a fun gathering with friends and family. Feel free to experiment with different fillings and toppings to suit your taste preferences.

Jerk Chicken Sliders

Ingredients:

- For the Jerk Chicken:
    - 1 pound boneless, skinless chicken breasts or thighs, cut into small pieces
    - ¼ cup jerk seasoning (store-bought or homemade)
    - 2 tablespoons olive oil
    - Salt and pepper, to taste
- For the Sliders:
    - Slider buns or small dinner rolls
    - Pineapple slices
    - Lettuce leaves
    - Sliced red onion
    - Sliced jalapeños (optional, for extra heat)
    - Mango salsa or pineapple salsa (optional, for topping)
    - Mayonnaise or jerk aioli (optional, for spreading)

Instructions:

1. Marinate the Jerk Chicken:
    - In a bowl, combine the jerk seasoning, olive oil, salt, and pepper to create a marinade.
    - Add the chicken pieces to the marinade and toss until evenly coated. Cover the bowl and refrigerate for at least 30 minutes, or preferably overnight, to allow the flavors to meld.
2. Cook the Jerk Chicken:
    - Heat a grill or grill pan over medium-high heat. Once hot, add the marinated chicken pieces to the grill.
    - Cook the chicken for 4-5 minutes on each side, or until fully cooked through and nicely charred. Make sure the internal temperature of the chicken reaches 165°F (74°C).
    - Once cooked, remove the chicken from the grill and let it rest for a few minutes.
3. Assemble the Sliders:
    - Slice the slider buns or dinner rolls in half horizontally.
    - Place a lettuce leaf on the bottom half of each bun.
    - Top with a piece of grilled jerk chicken.

- Add a pineapple slice on top of the chicken.
- Place a slice of red onion and sliced jalapeños (if using) on top of the pineapple.
- Spoon a dollop of mango salsa or pineapple salsa (if using) over the onions and jalapeños.
- Optionally, spread mayonnaise or jerk aioli on the top half of the bun before placing it on top of the slider.

4. Serve:
   - Serve the Jerk Chicken Sliders immediately, accompanied by additional salsa or aioli on the side if desired.
   - Enjoy the bold and spicy flavors of Jamaica in each bite!

These Jerk Chicken Sliders make a fantastic appetizer, snack, or main course for any occasion, from game day gatherings to summer cookouts. Adjust the level of spice according to your preference and enjoy the delicious fusion of flavors!

Tempura Chicken Waffle

Ingredients:

- For the Tempura Chicken:
    - 1 pound boneless, skinless chicken breasts or thighs, cut into bite-sized pieces
    - 1 cup all-purpose flour
    - 1 cup cornstarch
    - 1 teaspoon baking powder
    - 1 teaspoon salt
    - 1 cup cold sparkling water or club soda
    - Vegetable oil, for frying
- For the Waffles:
    - 2 cups all-purpose flour
    - 2 tablespoons sugar
    - 1 tablespoon baking powder
    - ½ teaspoon salt
    - 2 large eggs
    - 1 ¾ cups milk
    - ½ cup unsalted butter, melted
    - Cooking spray or extra butter for greasing the waffle iron

Instructions:

1. Prepare the Tempura Chicken:
    - In a large bowl, whisk together the all-purpose flour, cornstarch, baking powder, and salt.
    - Gradually add the cold sparkling water or club soda to the flour mixture, whisking until smooth.
    - Heat vegetable oil in a deep fryer or large pot to 350°F (175°C).
    - Dip the chicken pieces into the tempura batter, shaking off any excess batter.
    - Carefully place the battered chicken into the hot oil and fry in batches for 5-7 minutes, or until golden brown and cooked through. Remove the chicken from the oil and drain on a paper towel-lined plate.
2. Make the Waffles:
    - Preheat your waffle iron according to manufacturer's instructions.

- In a large mixing bowl, whisk together the flour, sugar, baking powder, and salt.
- In another bowl, whisk together the eggs, milk, and melted butter until well combined.
- Pour the wet ingredients into the dry ingredients and stir until just combined. Be careful not to overmix; a few lumps are okay.
- Lightly grease the waffle iron with cooking spray or brush with melted butter.
- Pour the batter onto the preheated waffle iron and cook according to the manufacturer's instructions, until the waffles are golden brown and crispy.

3. Assemble the Tempura Chicken Waffles:
    - Place a cooked waffle on a plate or serving platter.
    - Top with a generous portion of the tempura chicken pieces.
    - Drizzle with your favorite sauce, such as maple syrup, honey, or sriracha mayo.
    - Optionally, garnish with sliced green onions or sesame seeds for added flavor and texture.
4. Serve:
    - Serve the Tempura Chicken Waffles immediately, while the chicken is still hot and crispy.
    - Enjoy the delicious combination of crispy fried chicken and fluffy waffles in each bite!

These Tempura Chicken Waffles make a delightful and satisfying meal that's perfect for brunch, lunch, or dinner. Feel free to customize the toppings and sauces according to your taste preferences, and enjoy this unique fusion dish!

Kimchi Fries

Ingredients:

- 1 bag of frozen French fries (or homemade fries)
- 1 cup of kimchi, chopped
- 1 cup of shredded cheese (cheddar, mozzarella, or a blend)
- 2 green onions, thinly sliced
- 1 tablespoon of sesame seeds, for garnish
- 1 tablespoon of gochujang (Korean chili paste), for drizzling
- 2 tablespoons of mayonnaise (optional)
- 2 tablespoons of sour cream (optional)

Instructions:

1. Prepare the Fries:
    - If using frozen fries, cook them according to the package instructions until they are crispy and golden brown. If making homemade fries, fry or bake them until they are crispy.
2. Assemble the Kimchi Fries:
    - Once the fries are cooked, transfer them to a serving plate or platter.
    - Spread the chopped kimchi evenly over the fries.
    - Sprinkle the shredded cheese over the kimchi layer.
    - Place the plate of fries under the broiler in your oven for a few minutes until the cheese is melted and bubbly.
3. Garnish and Serve:
    - Remove the plate from the oven and sprinkle the sliced green onions and sesame seeds over the melted cheese.
    - Drizzle the gochujang over the top of the fries for added spice.
    - Optionally, mix the mayonnaise and sour cream together to create a creamy sauce, and drizzle it over the fries as well.
    - Serve the Kimchi Fries immediately while they are hot and enjoy the delicious blend of flavors!

Kimchi fries are a delightful and indulgent treat that combines the savory goodness of fries with the spicy kick of kimchi. They make a fantastic appetizer or snack for any occasion. Feel free to customize the toppings and garnishes according to your taste preferences.

Indian Samosa Tacos

Ingredients:

- For the Samosa Filling:
    - 2 large potatoes, boiled, peeled, and diced
    - 1 cup green peas, boiled or thawed if frozen
    - 1 tablespoon oil
    - 1 teaspoon cumin seeds
    - 1 small onion, finely chopped
    - 2 cloves garlic, minced
    - 1-inch piece of ginger, grated
    - 1 green chili, finely chopped (adjust to taste)
    - 1 teaspoon ground coriander
    - 1 teaspoon ground cumin
    - ½ teaspoon turmeric powder
    - ½ teaspoon garam masala
    - Salt to taste
    - 2 tablespoons chopped fresh cilantro (coriander leaves)
- For the Taco Shells:
    - Small soft tortillas or taco shells
- For Toppings:
    - Tamarind chutney
    - Mint chutney
    - Chopped onions
    - Chopped tomatoes
    - Chopped cilantro (coriander leaves)
    - Sev (crispy chickpea flour noodles)

Instructions:

1. Prepare the Samosa Filling:
    - Heat oil in a pan over medium heat. Add the cumin seeds and let them splutter.
    - Add the chopped onions and sauté until they turn translucent.
    - Add the minced garlic, grated ginger, and chopped green chili. Sauté for another minute.

- Add the ground coriander, ground cumin, turmeric powder, and garam masala. Stir well to combine.
- Add the diced potatoes and boiled green peas to the pan. Mix everything together gently.
- Season with salt to taste. Cook for a few minutes until the filling is heated through and the flavors meld.
- Remove from heat and stir in the chopped fresh cilantro. Set aside.

2. Assemble the Samosa Tacos:
   - Warm the tortillas or taco shells according to the package instructions.
   - Spoon a generous amount of the samosa filling into each tortilla or taco shell.
   - Top with chopped onions, tomatoes, cilantro, and sev.
   - Drizzle with tamarind chutney and mint chutney for extra flavor.
3. Serve:
   - Serve the Indian Samosa Tacos immediately while they're warm.
   - Enjoy the delightful fusion of Indian and Mexican flavors in each bite!

These Indian Samosa Tacos are perfect for a unique and delicious meal or as an appetizer for parties and gatherings. Feel free to customize the toppings and adjust the spice level according to your taste preferences.

Bulgogi Beef Sliders

Ingredients:

- For the Bulgogi Beef:
    - 1 pound beef sirloin or ribeye, thinly sliced
    - ¼ cup soy sauce
    - 2 tablespoons brown sugar
    - 2 tablespoons sesame oil
    - 2 cloves garlic, minced
    - 1 teaspoon grated ginger
    - 2 green onions, chopped
    - 1 tablespoon toasted sesame seeds
    - 1 tablespoon rice vinegar
    - 1 tablespoon mirin (optional)
    - 1 tablespoon vegetable oil, for cooking
- For the Sliders:
    - Slider buns or small dinner rolls
    - Thinly sliced cucumber
    - Shredded lettuce
    - Sliced red onion
    - Sriracha mayo or Korean chili paste (gochujang), for spreading
    - Additional sesame seeds and chopped green onions for garnish

Instructions:

1. Prepare the Bulgogi Beef:
    - In a bowl, combine the soy sauce, brown sugar, sesame oil, minced garlic, grated ginger, chopped green onions, toasted sesame seeds, rice vinegar, and mirin (if using). Mix well to make the marinade.
    - Add the thinly sliced beef to the marinade and toss until evenly coated. Cover and refrigerate for at least 1 hour, or overnight for best results.
    - Heat the vegetable oil in a large skillet or grill pan over medium-high heat. Once hot, add the marinated beef in a single layer.
    - Cook the beef for 2-3 minutes per side, or until it is caramelized and cooked through. Remove from heat and set aside.
2. Assemble the Sliders:
    - Slice the slider buns or dinner rolls in half horizontally.

- Spread a layer of Sriracha mayo or Korean chili paste (gochujang) on the bottom half of each bun.
- Place a portion of the cooked bulgogi beef on top of the mayo or chili paste.
- Top with thinly sliced cucumber, shredded lettuce, and sliced red onion.
- Sprinkle with additional toasted sesame seeds and chopped green onions for garnish.

3. Serve:
   - Place the top half of the buns over the fillings to form sliders.
   - Serve the Bulgogi Beef Sliders immediately, while they're warm and the flavors are fresh.
   - Enjoy the delicious fusion of Korean flavors in each bite!

These Bulgogi Beef Sliders are perfect for a party, game day, or any casual gathering. They're easy to make and bursting with savory, sweet, and tangy flavors. Feel free to customize the toppings and adjust the spice level to suit your taste preferences.

Sushi Nachos

Ingredients:

- For the Nachos:
    - 1 bag of tortilla chips
    - 1 cup cooked sushi rice, seasoned with rice vinegar and sugar
    - 1 cup imitation crab meat, shredded
    - 1 small cucumber, diced
    - 1 avocado, diced
    - 1/4 cup pickled ginger, chopped
    - 2 green onions, thinly sliced
    - 2 tablespoons sesame seeds, toasted
    - 1 nori sheet (seaweed), thinly sliced
- For the Spicy Mayo Sauce:
    - 1/4 cup mayonnaise
    - 1 tablespoon Sriracha sauce (adjust to taste)
    - 1 teaspoon sesame oil
    - 1 teaspoon soy sauce
- Optional Toppings:
    - Wasabi paste
    - Soy sauce
    - Masago (fish roe)
    - Furikake (Japanese seasoning)

Instructions:

1. Prepare the Spicy Mayo Sauce:
    - In a small bowl, whisk together the mayonnaise, Sriracha sauce, sesame oil, and soy sauce until well combined. Adjust the amount of Sriracha sauce to achieve your desired level of spiciness. Set aside.
2. Assemble the Nachos:
    - Arrange the tortilla chips on a large serving platter or baking sheet.
    - Scatter the cooked sushi rice evenly over the tortilla chips.
    - Sprinkle the shredded imitation crab meat, diced cucumber, and diced avocado over the rice layer.
    - Drizzle the spicy mayo sauce over the nachos according to your preference.

- Sprinkle the chopped pickled ginger, sliced green onions, and toasted sesame seeds over the nachos.
- Garnish with thinly sliced nori sheets on top for added flavor and presentation.

3. Optional Toppings:
    - If desired, you can add additional toppings such as wasabi paste, soy sauce, masago (fish roe), or furikake (Japanese seasoning) for extra flavor and texture.
4. Serve:
    - Serve the Sushi Nachos immediately, while the tortilla chips are still crispy and the toppings are fresh.
    - Enjoy the unique fusion of sushi flavors with the crunch of nachos!

These Sushi Nachos are perfect for parties, gatherings, or any occasion where you want to impress your guests with a creative and delicious appetizer. Feel free to customize the toppings and adjust the spiciness of the mayo sauce to suit your taste preferences.

Pad Thai Burrito

Ingredients:

- For the Pad Thai Filling:
    - 8 ounces rice noodles
    - 2 tablespoons vegetable oil
    - 2 cloves garlic, minced
    - 1 small onion, thinly sliced
    - 1 cup cooked chicken, shrimp, or tofu (optional)
    - 2 eggs, lightly beaten
    - 1 cup bean sprouts
    - 1/2 cup chopped green onions
    - 1/4 cup chopped peanuts
    - Lime wedges, for serving
- For the Pad Thai Sauce:
    - 1/4 cup soy sauce
    - 2 tablespoons tamarind paste
    - 2 tablespoons brown sugar
    - 1 tablespoon fish sauce
    - 1 teaspoon sriracha sauce (optional, adjust to taste)
- For the Burrito:
    - Large flour tortillas
    - Shredded lettuce
    - Sliced cucumber
    - Thinly sliced red bell pepper
    - Fresh cilantro leaves
    - Extra lime wedges

Instructions:

1. Prepare the Pad Thai Sauce:
    - In a small bowl, whisk together the soy sauce, tamarind paste, brown sugar, fish sauce, and sriracha sauce (if using) until well combined. Set aside.
2. Cook the Rice Noodles:

- Cook the rice noodles according to the package instructions until they are tender. Drain and rinse under cold water to stop the cooking process. Set aside.
3. Prepare the Pad Thai Filling:
    - Heat vegetable oil in a large skillet or wok over medium-high heat. Add the minced garlic and thinly sliced onion, and sauté until fragrant.
    - Add the cooked chicken, shrimp, or tofu (if using) to the skillet, and cook until heated through.
    - Push the ingredients to one side of the skillet, and pour the beaten eggs into the empty space. Scramble the eggs until cooked through, then mix them with the other ingredients in the skillet.
    - Add the cooked rice noodles and bean sprouts to the skillet, and pour the prepared Pad Thai sauce over the ingredients. Toss everything together until well coated and heated through.
    - Remove the skillet from heat, and stir in the chopped green onions and chopped peanuts.
4. Assemble the Burritos:
    - Warm the flour tortillas in a dry skillet or microwave until soft and pliable.
    - Place a portion of the Pad Thai filling in the center of each tortilla.
    - Top with shredded lettuce, sliced cucumber, thinly sliced red bell pepper, and fresh cilantro leaves.
    - Squeeze a lime wedge over the filling for an extra burst of flavor.
5. Roll the Burritos:
    - Fold the sides of the tortilla over the filling, then roll it up tightly from the bottom to form a burrito.
6. Serve:
    - Serve the Pad Thai Burritos immediately, with extra lime wedges on the side.
    - Enjoy the delicious fusion of Pad Thai flavors in a convenient handheld form!

These Pad Thai Burritos are perfect for a quick and satisfying meal that's packed with flavor. Customize the fillings according to your preferences, and get creative with your favorite toppings!

Banh Mi Tacos

Ingredients:

- For the Taco Filling:
    - 1 pound pork shoulder or pork belly, thinly sliced
    - 2 tablespoons soy sauce
    - 2 tablespoons fish sauce
    - 2 tablespoons honey or brown sugar
    - 2 cloves garlic, minced
    - 1 tablespoon grated ginger
    - 1 tablespoon vegetable oil
    - Salt and pepper, to taste
- For the Pickled Vegetables:
    - 1 carrot, julienned
    - 1 daikon radish, julienned
    - ½ cup rice vinegar
    - ¼ cup water
    - 2 tablespoons sugar
    - 1 teaspoon salt
- For the Toppings:
    - Thinly sliced cucumber
    - Sliced jalapeños
    - Fresh cilantro leaves
    - Sliced green onions
    - Sriracha mayo or mayonnaise mixed with Sriracha sauce
    - Lime wedges, for serving
- For Serving:
    - Small corn or flour tortillas

Instructions:

1. Marinate and Cook the Pork:
    - In a bowl, combine the soy sauce, fish sauce, honey or brown sugar, minced garlic, grated ginger, vegetable oil, salt, and pepper to make the marinade.
    - Add the thinly sliced pork to the marinade and toss until evenly coated. Cover and refrigerate for at least 30 minutes, or overnight for best results.

- Heat a skillet or grill pan over medium-high heat. Once hot, add the marinated pork slices and cook for 3-4 minutes per side, or until cooked through and caramelized. Remove from heat and set aside.
2. Prepare the Pickled Vegetables:
    - In a small saucepan, combine the rice vinegar, water, sugar, and salt. Bring to a boil, then remove from heat and let cool slightly.
    - Place the julienned carrot and daikon radish in a clean jar or bowl, and pour the vinegar mixture over them. Let them marinate for at least 30 minutes, or longer for stronger flavor.
3. Assemble the Banh Mi Tacos:
    - Warm the tortillas in a dry skillet or microwave until soft and pliable.
    - Place a few slices of cooked pork on each tortilla.
    - Top with pickled vegetables, thinly sliced cucumber, sliced jalapeños, fresh cilantro leaves, and sliced green onions.
    - Drizzle with Sriracha mayo or your favorite sauce for added flavor.
4. Serve:
    - Serve the Banh Mi Tacos immediately, accompanied by lime wedges for squeezing over the tacos.
    - Enjoy the delicious fusion of Vietnamese banh mi flavors in convenient taco form!

These Banh Mi Tacos are perfect for a fun and flavorful meal that's sure to impress. Customize the toppings according to your preferences, and enjoy the delicious blend of sweet, savory, tangy, and spicy flavors in each bite!

BBQ Pulled Jackfruit Sandwich

Ingredients:

- For the BBQ Pulled Jackfruit:
    - 2 cans young green jackfruit in water or brine, drained and rinsed
    - 1 tablespoon vegetable oil
    - 1 small onion, finely chopped
    - 2 cloves garlic, minced
    - 1 cup barbecue sauce (homemade or store-bought)
    - 1/2 cup vegetable broth or water
    - 1 tablespoon soy sauce or tamari
    - 1 tablespoon apple cider vinegar
    - 1 tablespoon brown sugar (optional)
    - Salt and pepper, to taste
- For Serving:
    - Burger buns or sandwich rolls
    - Coleslaw (optional)
    - Pickles (optional)
    - Sliced red onion (optional)

Instructions:

1. Prepare the Jackfruit:
    - Rinse the canned jackfruit under cold water and drain well. Pat dry with paper towels and remove the seeds and any tough core pieces.
    - Using your hands or a fork, shred the jackfruit into small, pulled-pork-like pieces.
2. Cook the BBQ Pulled Jackfruit:
    - Heat the vegetable oil in a large skillet over medium heat. Add the chopped onion and garlic, and sauté until softened and fragrant.
    - Add the shredded jackfruit to the skillet and cook for 5-7 minutes, stirring occasionally, until slightly browned.
    - In a small bowl, whisk together the barbecue sauce, vegetable broth or water, soy sauce or tamari, apple cider vinegar, and brown sugar (if using).
    - Pour the barbecue sauce mixture over the jackfruit in the skillet. Stir to combine and coat the jackfruit evenly with the sauce.

- Reduce the heat to low and let the jackfruit simmer for 15-20 minutes, stirring occasionally, until it's tender and has absorbed some of the sauce.
- Season with salt and pepper to taste.

3. Assemble the Sandwiches:
    - Toast the burger buns or sandwich rolls, if desired.
    - Place a generous amount of the BBQ pulled jackfruit on the bottom half of each bun.
    - Top with coleslaw, pickles, sliced red onion, or any other desired toppings.
    - Place the top half of the bun on top of the filling to complete the sandwiches.
4. Serve:
    - Serve the BBQ Pulled Jackfruit Sandwiches immediately, with extra barbecue sauce on the side if desired.
    - Enjoy the delicious and satisfying plant-based alternative to pulled pork sandwiches!

These BBQ Pulled Jackfruit Sandwiches are perfect for a meatless barbecue, picnic, or weeknight dinner. They're packed with flavor, protein, and fiber, making them a nutritious and satisfying option for vegetarians and meat-eaters alike.

www.ingramcontent.com/pod-product-compliance
Lightning Source LLC
LaVergne TN
LVHW081558060526
838201LV00054B/1946